At Issue

| The Opioid Crisis

Other Books in the At Issue Series

At Issue

| The Opioid Crisis

Sabine Cherenfant, Book Editor

GREENHAVEN
PUBLISHING

Published in 2020 by Greenhaven Publishing, LLC
353 3rd Avenue, Suite 255, New York, NY 10010

Copyright © 2020 by Greenhaven Publishing, LLC

First Edition

Articles in Greenhaven Publishing anthologies are often edited for length to meet page
requirements. In addition, original titles of these works are changed to clearly present
the main thesis and to explicitly indicate the author's opinion. Every effort is made to
ensure that Greenhaven Publishing accurately reflects the original intent of the authors.
Every effort has been made to trace the owners of the copyrighted material.

Cover image: Billion Photos/Shutterstock.com

Library of Congress Cataloging-in-Publication Data

Names: Cherenfant, Sabine, editor.
Title: The opioid crisis / Sabine Cherenfant, book editor [compiling editor].
Other titles: At issue
Description: First edition. | New York : Greenhaven Publishing, 2020. |
  Series: At issue | Audience: Grades 9 to 12. | Includes bibliographical
  references and index.
Identifiers: LCCN 2019003696| ISBN 9781534505247 (library bound) | ISBN
  9781534505254 (pbk.)
Subjects: LCSH: Opioid abuse—Juvenile literature. | Drug abuse—Juvenile
  literature.
Classification: LCC RC568.O45 O75 2020 | DDC 362.29/3—dc23
LC record available at https://lccn.loc.gov/2019003696

Manufactured in the United States of America

Website: http://greenhavenpublishing.com

Contents

Introduction

According to Vox senior reporter German Lopez "more Americans died of drug overdoses in 2016 than died in the entirety of the Vietnam War."[1] The United States has seen several drug epidemics through the span of its existence, but the opioid crisis has proven to be the most lethal, causing approximately 62,000 deaths in 2015 alone. Moreover, the National Institute on Drug Abuse estimates that 2.1 million Americans were addicted to prescription opioids as of 2016, and this rise in opioid addiction also caused a surge in HIV and Hepatitis C diagnoses.[2] This volume examines the history of the opioid crisis, its trajectory to becoming the worst drug crisis in the history of the United States, and the pros and cons of the potential solutions to curb the crisis.

Opioids are a type of drug used to mitigate pain. They help the brain forget about pain by attaching themselves to opioid receptors. According to Yvette Terrie of the *Pharmacy Times*, opioids have been recognized for their ability to lessen discomfort in patients with acute pain for centuries. In fact, Terrie adds that when taken correctly, opioids play a vital role for cancer patients and for those suffering from chronic pain. She writes: "The pain associated with cancer and other terminal illnesses should be treated aggressively to achieve adequate pain relief and often requires a multidisciplinary approach with individualized dosing."[3] This suggests that the problem with opioids is not the drugs themselves, but the fact that if they are mishandled or not administered correctly, they can lead to dependency.

Drugs that fall under the opiate category are fentanyl, codeine, hydrocodone, hydromorphone, morphine, methadone, oxycodone, and naloxone.[4] At the center of the epidemic is fentanyl, which is a powerful drug that has been increasingly produced illegally and is responsible for a surge in overdoses. For instance, between January 2017 and February 2017 in Montgomery County, Ohio, out of the one hundred deaths by drug overdose reported, ninety-nine of them were related to fentanyl.[5] Kristina Davis of the *San Diego Union-Tribune* describes this narcotic as "an incredibly potent synthetic opioid...[that] is regularly laced in counterfeit pills or other illicit drugs, often without knowledge of the users." She also adds that even the smallest amount can do a lot of damage.[6] Another drug at the center of this epidemic is heroin. Many of those addicted to opioids started on prescription opioids that were either badly administered or abused. When they could no longer obtain prescription drugs, they turned to heroin or other illegally produced opioids, which are more accessible.

The source of this epidemic can be traced back to the 1990s, when prescriptions for painkillers skyrocketed. The country's attitude toward pain changed, and it became normal to prescribe patients opioids for their pain as opposed to other alternative treatments like over-the-counter medications. This was due to a supposed scientific study that was actually performed by pharmaceutical companies, which asserted that the risk of opioid addiction was not significant. As a result, the restriction on opioid prescriptions became so relaxed that in 2012 alone 259 million opioids were prescribed. But as the prescriptions for opioids rose, so did the death toll.[7]

In her editorial for the *Washington Post* titled "A doctor's dilemma: Do I prescribe opioids?" Alison Block talked about the importance of prescribing opioids to patients with chronic pain. She asserted that the issue of whether opioids should be prescribed falls more in the grey area and varies case by case. Doctors deal with making intuitive decisions based on each patient's needs because opioids are still an important anesthetic agent for patients with severe pain. Yet the medical community's use of opioids can also contribute to the crisis, as evidenced by the issue of pain management facilities known as "pill mills." Based on a survey of two thousand people by the National Institute on Drug Abuse, pain management facilities are the third leading providers of opioid prescriptions after primary care physicians and specialty doctors.[8] The problem with pain management facilities is that many times they function as pill mills, defined by Pia Malbran of CBS as places where doctors prescribe narcotics without a medical cause. These clinics or pharmacies are illegal, and doctors that prescribe opioid drugs without a valid medical reason can be charged with a felony offense.[9]

Heroin is also tied to this epidemic because of how easy it is to obtain it. The drug itself is derived from morphine, and besides being absorbed as an injection, it can also be inhaled through the nose or through smoking.[10] As Lopez explained in his article "The Opioid Epidemic, Explained," 75 percent of heroin users were first opioid drug abusers. Many of the patients who became addicted to opioids ended up moving to fentanyl and heroin when they no longer had access to medication or when they needed a more powerful effect.[11]

Many potential solutions are currently being considered to fight the opioid epidemic. When looking at the crack epidemic of the late 1980s, there was a heavy focus on putting drug users behind bars. The way this crisis was addressed is still heavily debated today, in large part because it was believed to have targeted mostly marginalized communities. The current opioid epidemic has brought to the forefront the need to treat drug abuse as a disease in order to give those addicted to drugs the confidence and resources they need to seek help.

On October 26, 2017, President Donald Trump issued a statement declaring the opioid crisis a health emergency. In this briefing, the Trump administration explained that by declaring the opioid crisis a public health emergency, it would make medical support for people suffering from opioid and heroin addiction more accessible. Under his administration, $1 billion has been assigned to fighting drug addiction. The administration also established the President's Commission on Combatting Drug Addiction and the Opioid Crisis, which was tasked with assessing the issue and with helping find a more effective way to end the epidemic. The Trump administration's proposed solution to this epidemic is to allocate more money to first responders, preventive care, and to communities that are most at risk.[12]

As part of its solution, the Trump administration also wants to end the over-prescription of opioids and cut down the supply of drugs. This required deep investigation that has already had clear effects, as it has led to the dismantling of a major illicit drug producer in China. According to Paul Knierim, the DEA's deputy chief of operations, "Chinese chemical companies…[are] one of the predominant sources for illicit forms of… [fentanyl, an opioid]."[13] Nevertheless, his administration has received criticism for its delayed response to the crisis. Many experts lament the lack of funding provided by the administration and argue that the plan will not have enough of an impact.[14]

The opioid crisis is a vast subject. Each state tries to cope with the epidemic in the best way possible, introducing new laws and making available different programs to provide help to those suffering from drug use disorder. As expected, each potential solution comes with pros and cons. For instance, some cities want to introduce the concept of safe injection sites to the United States—a program that is already available in Canada, Europe, and Australia—but the federal government opposes it, making it difficult to test its efficacy. The benefit of safe injections sites is the safety net they provide to drug users, since they offer clean needles, reduce the risk of infections, and prevent deaths from overdose.[15] Yet concerns remain about whether these sites encourage drug use in the long run. Do they address the most important question for drug abuse: how do you end it once and for all? The viewpoints in *At Issue: The Opioid Crisis* will help students understand the history of this crisis and the opposing perspectives on how to end it. Based on the history of opioids and the different causes that have contributed to the crisis, how should this issue be addressed?

Notes

1. Lopez, German. "In One Year, Drug Overdoses Killed More Americans Than the Entire Vietnam War Did," *Vox*, June 8, 2017. Accessed September 27, 2018. https://www.vox.com/policy-and-politics/2017/6/6/15743986/opioid-epidemic-overdose-deaths-2016

2. "Medications to Treat Opioid Use Disorder," National Institute on Drug Abuse, June 2018. Accessed September 27, 2018. https://www.drugabuse.gov/publications/research-reports/medications-to-treat-opioid-addiction/overview

3. Terrie, Yvette C. "An Overview of Opioids" *Pharmacy Times*, June 13, 2011. Accessed September 27, 2018. https://www.pharmacytimes.com/publications/issue/2011/june2011/an-overview-of-opioids

4. Bhargava, Hansa D. "Opioid (Narcotic) Pain Medications," WebMD, September 20, 2018. Accessed September 27, 2018. https://www.webmd.com/pain-management/guide/narcotic-pain-medications#1

5. Katz, Josh. "Drug Deaths in America Are Rising Faster Than Ever," *New York Times*, June 5, 2017. Accessed September 27, 2018. https://www.nytimes.com/interactive/2017/06/05/upshot/opioid-epidemic-drug-overdose-deaths-are-rising-faster-than-ever.html

6. Davis, Kristina. "Arrest Made in La Jolla Man's Fentanyl Overdose Death," *San Diego Union-Tribune*, October 10, 2018. Accessed October 10, 2018. http://www.sandiegouniontribune.com/news/courts/sd-me-fentanyl-death-20181010-story.html

7. Block, Alison. "A Doctor's Dilemma: Do I Prescribe Opioids?" *Washington Post*, June 10, 2016. Accessed October 8, 2018. https://www.washingtonpost.com/opinions/a-doctors-dilemma-do-i-prescribe-opioids/2016/06/10/be4bb51e-2c31-11e6-b5db-e9bc84a2c8e4_story.html?noredirect=on&utm_term=.26887a42f881

8. "America's Pill Mills: A Look into the Prescription Opioid Problem," DrugAbuse.com, October 10, 2018. https://drugabuse.com/featured/americas-pill-mills/

9. Malbran, Pia. "What's a Pill Mill?" *CBS News*, May 31, 2007. Accessed October 10, 2018. https://www.cbsnews.com/news/whats-a-pill-mill/

10. "Heroin." National Institute on Drug Abuse, June 2018. Accessed October 10, 2018. https://www.drugabuse.gov/publications/drugfacts/heroin#ref

11. Lopez, German. "The Opioid Epidemic, Explained," *Vox*, December 21, 2017. Accessed October 10, 2018. https://www.vox.com/science-and-health/2017/8/3/16079772/opioid-epidemic-drug-overdoses

12. "President Donald J. Trump is Taking Action on Drug Addiction and the Opioid Crisis," Whitehouse.gov, October 26. 2017. Accessed October 10, 2018. https://www.whitehouse.gov/briefings-statements/president-donald-j-trump-taking-action-drug-addiction-opioid-crisis/

13. McCausland, Phil and Tom Winter. "China and the United States come to agreement at G-20 summit around fentanyl," *NBC News*, December 2, 2018. Accessed January 23, 2019. https://www.nbcnews.com/news/us-news/china-united-states-come-agreement-around-fentanyl-n942766

14. Lopez, German. "Elizabeth Warren Wants Answers About Trump's "Pathetic" Response to The Opioid Epidemic," *Vox*, July 19, 2018. Accessed October 10, 2018. https://www.vox.com/policy-and-politics/2018/7/19/17590434/elizabeth-warren-trump-opioid-epidemic

15. Gordon, Elana. "What's the Evidence That Supervised Drug Injection Sites Save Lives?" National Public Radio, September 7, 2018. Accessed October 12, 2018. https://www.npr.org/sections/health-shots/2018/09/07/645609248/whats-the-evidence-that-supervised-drug-injection-sites-save-lives

1

What Is the Opioid Crisis?

Sarah E. Ludwig

Sarah Ludwig is a writer, editor, and business manager at Blue Zebra Media.

In order to consider possible solutions to the opioid crisis, it is essential to first understand what it is. This involves looking at the statistics that show its growth over the years and its wide-reaching impacts today, as well as some of the explanations for why it is occurring. This viewpoint also offers practical information about how to personally avoid getting sucked into the opioid crisis and how to identify signs of opioid addiction in oneself or others.

O pioids are everywhere in the news. Celebrities are often entering rehab to kick their addictions to painkillers or suffering overdoses from prescription opioids or heroin. The opioid epidemic doesn't just affect the rich and famous though. The Centers for Disease Control and Prevention (CDC) reports that the death toll from opioid overdoses, including heroin, synthetic opioids like fentanyl, and prescription opioids such as OxyContin and Vicodin, has quadrupled since 1999.[1] In 2015, an estimated 2 million people 12 or older in the United States had a pain reliever use disorder.[2] Heroin use is way up too, affecting nearly every demographic group.[3]

"The Opioid Crisis in America: An Overview," by Sarah E. Ludwig, Calvary Healing Center. Reprinted by permission.

These days, drug overdoses cause more deaths than car accidents. In 2015, 52,404 people died from a drug overdose, with a sobering 63% of these deaths involving opioids.[4] The number of drug deaths in 2016 is believed to be more than 59,000.[5] Compare this to car accidents, which took an estimated 40,200 lives in 2016.[6]

But what's fueling the epidemic? Why the drastic increase in opioid prescriptions, opioid use disorders and deaths from overdose? Why has heroin use skyrocketed? There are no simple answers to these questions.

Driving Factors Behind the Opioid Epidemic

Opioids Are Overprescribed

This is perhaps the single biggest cause of the opioid crisis. Sales for prescription opioids such as oxycodone, hydrocodone and methadone have almost quadrupled since 1999,[7] and close to half of all deaths from opioid overdose involve a prescribed opioid,[8] according to the CDC. In 2012, 12 states had more opioid prescriptions than they did people.[9]

Opioids May Not Be Prescribed Correctly

When this happens, the drug may create a feeling of euphoria in the patient, which can then lead to misuse, dependence or a full blown opioid use disorder. People with opioid use disorder are 40 times more likely to be addicted to heroin.[10]

A Lack of Physician Education

A 2016 survey by the National Safety Council of 201 board-certified internal medicine and family doctors revealed that 99% of the doctors surveyed prescribe opioids for longer than the three-day period recommended by the CDC and that 74% believe that oxycodone and morphine, both opioids, are the most effective treatments for pain.[11] However, evidence shows that other pain relievers, particularly ibuprofen, are actually more effective than opioids.[12]

Though this survey involved a small sample of physicians, it reveals the need for physician education when it comes to prescribing opioids and looking for other alternatives to treat pain. Interestingly, the CDC recommends only using opioids for patients in active cancer treatment, those who have serious illnesses and patients nearing death.[13] If opioids are used for chronic pain, the CDC has published guidelines to help physicians prescribe them as safely and effectively as possible, noting that opioids should be used sparingly and for as short a time as possible, at the lowest effective dose.[14]

Graduating from Prescription Opioids to Heroin

The CDC reports that 45 percent of heroin users were also addicted to prescription opioids.[15] Heroin tends to be easier to get and less expensive than prescription opioids. It's usually more potent too, and since it's not monitored by a physician, it has a higher risk of overdose and addiction. People who have other substance use disorders are also more likely to become addicted to heroin.[16]

The Availability of Heroin

It's clear that Mexican cartels are now bringing more heroin than cocaine or marijuana to the United States.[17] The amount of heroin confiscated at the US border quadrupled between 2008 and 2013.[18] Mexico's heroin production increased sixfold between 2005 and 2009, making the availability of the drug higher than ever.[19] What's unclear is if heroin use is on the rise because of its easy availability or if it's easily available because of the increased demand.[20]

What You Can Do

- If you need surgery or other short-term pain relief, talk to your doctor about your pain management options. Be aware that using opioids involves the risk of addiction or accidental overdose. Your best bet is to use over-the-counter pain relievers such as acetaminophen and ibuprofen, which have been shown to be more effective at relieving pain than opioids anyway. You may also benefit from physical therapy and/or exercise.[21]

- If you are prescribed an opioid, ask your doctor to give you the lowest needed dose for the least amount of time and be sure to follow the instructions you're given. Never take more than you have been prescribed as this can result in accidental overdose or lead to addiction. Be sure to dispose of any leftover medication safely and never share it with anyone else.
- If you suffer from chronic pain, opioids may be a part of your pain management plan. You will need to be monitored closely by your doctor and it's important that you follow prescribing instructions exactly.[22] Work with your doctor to supplement or replace opioids with other options such as exercise, Cognitive Behavioral Therapy (CBT) and pain relievers that are not opioids.[23]
- Talk to your kids about opioid misuse and addiction. In the last decade, heroin use has more than doubled among 18- to 25-year-olds.[24]

Signs of Opioid Use Disorder

Physical symptoms of opioid use include the following:

- feeling high (euphoria)
- drowsiness
- slurred speech
- confusion
- difficulty breathing
- nausea
- vomiting
- itchy skin
- constipation
- small pupils[25]

According to the Substance Abuse and Mental Health Services Administration (SAMHSA), symptoms of an opioid use disorder include the following:

- feeling a powerful urge to take opioids

- building up a tolerance to them, meaning that you need larger quantities in order to get the same effects
- being unable to stop using opioids
- having difficulty at work and/or in social situations
- potential legal trouble due to your opioid use
- devoting a large chunk of your time to getting and/or using opioids
- experiencing withdrawal symptoms when you try to stop or decrease the amount of opioids you use[26]

Treatment for Opioid Use Disorder

If you or a loved one show signs of having an opioid use disorder, you are not alone. Comprehensive treatment is available at Calvary Healing Center for both the opioid addiction and any underlying psychological or emotional conditions that may be fueling the drug use.

It's a complex problem with no immediate solution, but the opioid epidemic doesn't appear to be going away anytime soon. Educating yourself and others about the risks of using opioids, whether by prescription or illicitly, can help reduce the number of people who misuse or abuse opioids.

Sources

1. https://www.cdc.gov/drugoverdose/data/overdose.html

2. https://www.samhsa.gov/data/sites/default/files/NSDUH-FFR1-2015Rev1/NSDUH-FFR1-2015Rev1/NSDUH-FFR1-2015Rev1/NSDUH-National%20Findings-REVISED-2015.pdf, page 25

3. https://www.cdc.gov/drugoverdose/data/heroin.html

4. https://www.cdc.gov/mmwr/volumes/65/wr/mm655051e1.htm

5. https://www.nytimes.com/interactive/2017/06/05/upshot/opioid-epidemic-drug-overdose-deaths-are-rising-faster-than-ever.html

6. https://www.nytimes.com/2017/02/15/business/highway-traffic-safety.html

7. https://www.cdc.gov/drugoverdose/epidemic/index.html

8. https://www.cdc.gov/drugoverdose/data/overdose.html

9. http://www.pbs.org/wgbh/frontline/article/how-bad-is-the-opioid-epidemic/

10. https://www.cdc.gov/vitalsigns/heroin/index.html

11. http://www.nsc.org/NewsDocuments/2016/Doctor-Survey-press-briefing-32416.pdf, page 5

12. http://www.nsc.org/RxDrugOverdoseDocuments/Evidence-Efficacy-Pain-Medications.pdf

13. https://www.cdc.gov/drugoverdose/prescribing/guideline.html

14. https://www.cdc.gov/drugoverdose/prescribing/providers.html

15. https://www.cdc.gov/vitalsigns/heroin/index.html

16. https://www.cdc.gov/vitalsigns/heroin/index.html

17. https://www.usatoday.com/story/news/world/2016/11/17/heroin-mexican-drug-cartel/94032394/

18. https://www.cdc.gov/drugoverdose/data/heroin.html

19. https://www.drugabuse.gov/publications/research-reports/relationship-between-prescription-drug-abuse-heroin-use/increased-drug-availability-associated-increased-use-overdose

20. https://www.drugabuse.gov/publications/research-reports/relationship-between-prescription-drug-abuse-heroin-use/heroin-use-driven-by-its-low-cost-high-availability 21. https://www.cdc.gov/drugoverdose/prescribing/patients.html

22. https://www.cdc.gov/drugoverdose/prescribing/patients.html

23. https://www.cdc.gov/drugoverdose/prescribing/providers.html

24. https://www.cdc.gov/vitalsigns/heroin/index.html

25. http://www.webmd.com/mental-health/addiction/painkillers-and-addiction-narcotic-abuse#2-2

26. https://www.samhsa.gov/disorders/substance-use

2

The History and Potential Future of the Opioid Crisis

Amie L. Severino, Arash Shadfar, Joshua K. Hakimian, Oliver Crane, Ganeev Singh, Keith Heinzerling, and Wendy M. Walwyn

Amie L. Severino, Joshua K. Hakimian, Oliver Crane, Ganeev Singh, Keith Heinzerling, and Wendy M. Walwyn are scholars at the David Geffen School of Medicine at the University of California –Los Angeles. Arash Shadfar is a doctor at Western University of Health Sciences.

The rise of opioid overdoses results from a complex history related to the nature of the drug, as well as the misleading studies and advertising campaigns that resulted in a large number of opioid prescriptions. The euphoria effect that opioids release when consumed contribute greatly to the surge of opioid addiction. In this viewpoint, the authors urge new opioid medication that does not result in this euphoria. Another notable part of the crisis is the amount of money that pharmaceutical companies make from it, which should be curbed going forward.

"Pain Therapy Guided by Purpose and Perspective in Light of the Opioid Epidemic," by Amie L. Severino, Arash Shadfar, Joshua K. Hakimian, Oliver Crane, Ganeev Singh, Keith Heinzerling, and Wendy M. Walwyn, Frontiers in Psychiatry, April 23, 2018, https://www.frontiersin.org/articles/10.3389/fpsyt.2018.00119/full. Licensed under CC BY 4.0 International.

Prescription opioid misuse is an ongoing and escalating epidemic. Although these pharmacological agents are highly effective analgesics prescribed for different types of pain, opioids also induce euphoria, leading to increasing diversion and misuse. Opioid use and related mortalities have developed in spite of initial claims that OxyContin, one of the first opioids prescribed in the USA, was not addictive in the presence of pain. These claims allayed the fears of clinicians and contributed to an increase in the number of prescriptions, quantity of drugs manufactured, and the unforeseen diversion of these drugs for non-medical uses. Understanding the history of opioid drug development, the widespread marketing campaign for opioids, the immense financial incentive behind the treatment of pain, and vulnerable socioeconomic and physical demographics for opioid misuse give perspective on the current epidemic as an American-born problem that has expanded to global significance. In light of the current worldwide opioid epidemic, it is imperative that novel opioids are developed to treat pain without inducing the euphoria that fosters physical dependence and addiction. We describe insights from preclinical findings on the properties of opioid drugs that offer insights into improving abuse-deterrent formulations. One finding is that the ability of some agonists to activate one pathway over another, or agonist bias, can predict whether several novel opioid compounds bear promise in treating pain without causing reward among other off-target effects. In addition, we outline how the pharmacokinetic profile of each opioid contributes to their potential for misuse and discuss the emergence of mixed agonists as a promising pipeline of opioid-based analgesics. These insights from preclinical findings can be used to more effectively identify opioids that treat pain without causing physical dependence and subsequent opioid abuse.

Oxycodone and Oxycontin at the Center of the Prescription Opioid Epidemic

The History of Oxycodone Treatment of Chronic Non-Cancer Pain

Oxycodone, a semisynthetic opioid, was first formulated in 1916 from thebaine, a chemical found in opium poppy plants. The drug was first marketed as a less addictive alternative to "narcotic" drugs, such as morphine and heroin, which were typically prescribed to patients as an analgesic in the early 1900s. Oxycodone was first released in the USA in 1939 by Merck as a combination drug containing scopolamine, oxycodone, and ephedrine, but was discontinued in 1987. Purdue Pharma then developed an extended-release formulation of oxycodone, called OxyContin. The FDA approved OxyContin in 1995, noting that the reduced frequency of dosing was the only advantage of OxyContin over regular oxycodone. This drug was aggressively marketed by Purdue Pharma for opioid-based management of moderate-to-severe cancer and non-cancer pain where the use of an opioid analgesic was considered appropriate for more than a few days. Purdue used an aggressive marketing strategy to target-specific physicians, particularly those with less time to evaluate patients and often with less training in pain-management techniques. This led to more than half of the total OxyContin prescriptions being written by primary care physicians rather than pain specialists. In addition, direct-to-consumer pharmaceutical advertising, allowed only in the USA and New Zealand, has contributed to mass consumer awareness of the availability of these drugs with a demonstrated influence on the prescribing practice of physicians. This aggressive physician directed marketing, as well as direct-to-consumer marketing, has become a benchmark for the marketing of opioids.

The Financial Incentive for Prescription Opioid Distribution

The Purdue-Frederick company first marketed MsContin (morphine sulfate) as an extended-release opioid-containing formula to treat pain in terminal cancer patients. MsContin generated $475 million in sales over a decade. After the Sackler brothers acquired Purdue-Frederick and rebranded the company as Purdue Pharma, they released OxyContin, which generated $45 million in sales in just the first year after its release in 1996. By 2001, the annual revenue from OxyContin sales reached $1.1 billion and rose to $2.528 billion by 2014 in the USA alone.

Currently, the Purdue Pharma company is 100% owned by members of the Sackler family, who are worth $13 billion and ranked as the 19th wealthiest family in the USA in 2016. In addition to Purdue Pharma and other Sackler holdings, there are several other companies manufacturing oxycodone and related opioid compounds to fill the 259 million annual prescriptions written to patients in the USA, generating an additional $11 billion in opioid sales annually in 2011. These include Abbot Labs, Novartis, Teva, Pfizer, Endo Pharmaceuticals, Impax, Actavis, Sandoz, Janssen Pharmaceuticals, etc. Together, these figures demonstrate the significant financial incentive pharmaceutical companies have to market opioid compounds despite growing concerns of the abuse liability and safety of these drugs.

Recognition of the Abuse Liability of Oxycodone and OxyContin

OxyContin was marketed as a delayed-release formulation allowing 12 h of continuous analgesia with fewer side effects than other opioid-based analgesics if used as directed. This formulation was promising in that the delayed-release would enable patients to sleep through the night, improving the standard of care for chronic pain patients at the time. However, this drug has been widely misused for non-medical purposes. At the time of the release of OxyContin in 1996, it was already known that 68% of an OxyContin tablet could be extracted by crushing the tablet. Since the first published reports of OxyContin abuse in 2000, public awareness of its abuse liability has grown. Indeed, Purdue-Frederick, a holding of Purdue Pharma, paid $470 million dollars in fines to federal and state agencies and $130 million of payments in civil suits due to the misbranding of OxyContin as non-addictive in 2007. Three executives of Purdue Pharma also pleaded guilty to OxyContin misbranding charges and paid $34.5 million in fines. By early 2017, there were daily reports of the diversion and misuse of prescription opioids with a number of states and counties across the country filing suit against five pharmaceutical companies, including Purdue. The plaintiffs in these suits claimed that the aggressive marketing campaign of opioid compounds is founded on fraudulent assertions of the safety of these drugs and that this misinformation has contributed to the ongoing opioid crisis. Purdue has responded to these claims by emphasizing that opioids are essential in pain management and that their extended-release abuse-deterrent formulations are evidence of their drive to reduce the diversion of OxyContin. In 2018, Purdue stated it will no longer advertise directly to American doctors, a measure that will hopefully reduce over-prescription of opioids.

The Patterns of Prescription Opioid Misuse and Overdose Mortalities Worldwide

The incidence of lifetime OxyContin abuse in the USA increased from 0.1% in 1999 to 0.4% in 2001. By 2013, over 1,000 Americans were treated daily in emergency departments for prescription opioid misuse and in 2014, 4.3 million people used prescription opioids for non-medical reasons. This trend was also seen in the number of deaths attributed to oxycodone, which increased from 14 cases in 1998 to ~14,000 cases in 2006 and 18,000 in 2015. Although not of the same magnitude and somewhat delayed, this increase in opioid abuse and mortality is also occurring in other countries. In Australia, oxycodone-related deaths increased sevenfold between 2001 and 2011. In Finland, opioid mortalities increased from 9.5% of all drug overdose deaths in 2000 to 32.4% in 2008, and data from Brazil, China, and the Middle East show similar increases in opioid diversion. In the United Kingdom, although tramadol and methadone are misused over oxycodone, the pattern of opioid misuse shows a similar increase to the USA albeit on a smaller scale. While Americans consume 80% of the global opioid supply and 99% of the global hydrocodone supply and the number of overdose mortalities is considerably higher in the USA, the opioid epidemic is growing worldwide.

The Most Vulnerable Populations

The incidence of opioid overdose mortality in the USA shows three hotspots: (1) the Appalachian states of Kentucky, Virginia, West Virginia, Pennsylvania, and Ohio, (2) the Northeast states of Maine, New Hampshire, and Rhode Island, and (3) the Southwest states of Nevada, Utah, New Mexico, and Arizona. This could be related to the demographics of these areas and the prescribing habits of the local medical professionals and pharmacies. Within all of these affected areas, opioid-related deaths are predominately Caucasians of middle age and are a result of drug overdose, alcohol-related disease, suicide, and psychiatric disorders. This has resulted in the first decline in life expectancy in the USA since 1993. This has been highlighted in a series of articles that describe this population as subject to the "deaths of despair" and a "toxic stress" response to benign early-life events.

The primary factor contributing to these "deaths of despair" is the collapse of the white high-school educated working class from its heyday of the 1970s. This population's struggles in the job market in early adulthood became more difficult over time and are accompanied by health and personal issues that contribute to an increased morbidity from chronic pain, and physical and mental health disorders including opioid use disorder [OUD]. The (USA) National Bureau of Economic Research found that for every 1% increase in unemployment, there is a 3.6% increase in opioid-related deaths, suggesting that macroeconomic conditions have influence over national drug misuse. Considering the global economic aftershocks of the USA's recession, we suggest that global economic recession contributed to the developing international opioid epidemic. To this point, a meta-analysis of research published from 1995 to 2015 in South America, the Caribbean, Europe, Asia, the USA, and Australia suggests that economic depression causes mental health issues that exacerbate illicit drug use. Case and Deaton additionally report that the use of prescription opioids did not create the vulnerable American profile, but the ease of availability of these compounds and the difficulty in treating opioid misuse in a depressed economy has inflamed the "sea of despair" that extends across the USA.

Addressing Chronic Pain in the Midst of the Opioid Epidemic
It is clear that mass production, marketing, and prescription of opioids for pain treatment has contributed to the opioid epidemic in vulnerable demographics, characterized by mental health disorders, socioeconomic challenges, and susceptibility to occupational injury. We discuss the interplay of mental health, pain, and depression, and how these factors contribute to the misuse and addiction of prescription opioids. One of the key marketing claims of pharmaceutical companies was that the presence of pain is protective against opioid misuse. The evidence for this claim is shockingly limited due to evolving diagnostic criterion for opioid misuse and does not account for the influence of mental health on opioid misuse behavior in the pain state. This gives us perspective toward treating pain with the intent to limit the pro-addiction properties and off-target effects of future pharmaceuticals to decrease opioid dependence in the chronic pain state. We look to insights from behavioral research on addiction and reward, and then to mechanistic research on the pharmacokinetic and signaling properties on opioids to address these issues.

[...]

Why Are Opioids so Addictive?
The motivation to continue taking drugs in spite of adverse consequences can be explained by several concurrent theories. The Opponent Process theory results from a balance between two valuationally opposite components, a loss of function within the

reward-mediating dopaminergic circuits and an increased function of stress-related circuitry involving the extended amygdala, the kappa/dynorphin opioid and corticotrophin-signaling systems. The latter system becomes hyperactive during opioid dependence and manifests as increased anxiety and aggressive behaviors. Another, co-occurring theory of the motivation behind continued drug use is the Incentive Sensitization theory that proposes an increase in drug-paired cues with chronic drug taking. Together, these systems drive drug-seeking behavior that is a product of (1) a decrease in positive outcome coupled with the promise and pull of drug-associated cues and (2) an increase in dysphoria between drug exposures and during withdrawal. This is particularly relevant for opioids as these compounds induce a tolerance to repeated exposures of the same dose of the drug. This leads to (1) an escalating intake of opioids over time resulting in compulsive opioid-taking behaviors, (2) increasing dependence, and (3) increasing negative affect seen in the absence of the drug that together culminate in further dysregulation of the reward system.

The negative affective state of depression and anxiety associated with chronic pain can be relieved temporarily by the analgesic and euphoric properties of acute opioid use, which contributes to their abuse liability in the chronic pain state. However, both pain and opioid use create a new homeostasis in the reward and stress-related pathways, an example of which can be seen in chronic pain patients who misuse opioids and also fail to show a positive affect from natural rewards. Preclinical studies in rodent models have been able to examine the interaction between pain and opioids at several levels. Pain does not affect the number of low doses of opioid infusions (of heroin, morphine, and oxycodone) earned in a self-administration model of drug-seeking behavior but does increase heroin self-administration to binge levels at higher doses and during prolonged access to the drug. By contrast, pain reduces the self-administration of fentanyl, a shorter-acting but highly efficacious opioid that rapidly crosses the blood–brain barrier (BBB). Pain also increases drug (morphine)-seeking behavior when the drug is no longer available. This result suggests that the abuse liability of opioids in the chronic pain state is not directly motivated by analgesia-seeking and intensifies when the drug is no longer available yet drug-associated cues and environmental stimuli are present. Together, these preclinical findings suggests that chronic pain produces a vulnerability to addiction-like behavior, bearing a similarity to the behavior of opioid addicts in chronic pain who are more likely to relapse once tapering off a maintenance buprenorphine naloxone treatment.

[...]

3

Drug Consumption Facilities Can Provide a Better Solution to the Opioid Epidemic

Jarrett Zigon

Jarrett Zigon teaches anthropology at the University of Virginia. He is also the author of the book A War on People: Drug User Politics and a New Ethics of Community.

Zigon believes that the best way to fight the opioid crisis is to focus on building communities. For instance, Canada is the first country in North America to legalize consumption sites for people suffering from drug addiction disorder. There, drug users have access to sterile needles and to trained professionals if something were to go wrong during injection. The purpose behind this initiative is to reduce the damages of drug use and to make it easier for drug users to transition out of this behavior when they decide to do so.

How should we address the opioid crisis? Perhaps we should ask those with the most experience of it—drug users. Having spoken to hundreds of drug users over the last 12 years as an ethnographic researcher, one thing made clear to me no matter where I go is that the best way to address problematic drug use is not through law and order but through care and community.

Perhaps the best example of a community-orientated approach to drug addiction can be found in Vancouver's Downtown Eastside neighbourhood, where organisations of active and former drug users and their allies responded to a drug epidemic in the 1990s with a focus on community-building and local revitalisation. When I visited in 2013, I witnessed first-hand how the scheme was transforming the lives of people living there. Small businesses and social enterprises, such as the community bank Pigeon Park Savings, had been created to offer employment and services to active drug users. There was a significant increase in social and affordable housing, several health—including mental health —facilities, and abundant community events open to public —including musical concerts. All of these various projects are supported by mixture of public funding, won by campaigners, and private donations and non-profit grants.

None of this would have been possible without the establishment of Insite, the first legally sanctioned safe consumption facility in North America. These facilities provide a space for people to consume pre-obtained drugs in controlled settings, under the supervision of trained staff, and with access to sterile injecting equipment. When Insite was first established in 2003, the Downtown Eastside had been home to hundreds of overdose deaths over the previous decade. In two years the fatal overdose rate decreased by 35%—then the fentanyl crisis hit. As in cities and small towns across the United States and Canada, many Downtown Eastsiders are now scrambling to respond to this latest drug-war exacerbated crisis. The difference is that because of the twenty-year-long political activism led by active and former drug users, the Downtown Eastside has the broadest and most integrated harm reduction infrastructure in the world from which to respond.

Harm reduction is a public health approach to drug use that begins from the nonjudgmental position that some people use drugs, those people will continue to use drugs until they decide to make a change, and until then certain measures should be taken to reduce the potential harm they cause themselves and others. The most common harm reduction measures are syringe exchange and substitution therapy (e.g. methadone). But perhaps the most effective one is safe consumption facilities like Insite. The facts bear this out: not only did overdose deaths radically decrease in the Downtown Eastside once Insite was opened, but so have they anywhere else in the world such facilities exist.

What makes the Downtown Eastside different from these other locations—and as a result, a global model for addressing opioid crises—is that harm reduction in the neighbourhood goes way beyond syringe exchange, substitution therapy, safe consumption facilities, and most recently heroin prescription. All of this is a great foundation for addressing opioid crises, but what the drug-using activists and their allies recognised from the very beginning is that it simply is not enough. Most people begin using hardcore drugs like heroin for a reason: sometimes to alleviate physical pain, and commonly to relieve emotional and mental pain. But too often the underlying condition shared by many of these users is a deep sense of isolation and loneliness, which is likely the result of social and economic precarity and anxiety. As one of the early Downtown Eastside activists Dean Wilson put it: "addiction is a disease of loneliness."

The real success of the Vancouver model is that it addresses this loneliness. This is what Teresa, one of the workers at a Downtown Eastside social enterprise who also happens to use drugs, described to me as giving people opportunities to become connected. When Teresa arrived in the neighbourhood she had been homeless, using drugs, and doing sex work for several years. Despite years of being uncared for, harassed by the police, and essentially left to die, Teresa was welcomed in the Downtown Eastside, where she easily found a safe and well-maintained single-occupancy-room in which to live, a social enterprise job that paid a fair wage and adjusted to the vicissitudes of her schedule, and most importantly she found people who cared about her as a person no matter her drug using habits.

What Teresa found in the Downtown Eastside was a community of what I call "attuned care," and this community was built by organisations of active and former drug users and their allies.

Attuned care is a kind of care that doesn't try to turn someone into something they are not, but rather cares for them as they are. This is another way of articulating the harm reduction motto of "meeting people where they are at." The magic of attuned care is that it often opens possibilities for the person given care to become someone who is themselves more caring, connected, and responsible to others. For example, though still an active drug user, Teresa now lives in her own apartment in a quiet neighborhood near Vancouver's Stanley Park, where she is writing a book on her experiences as a homeless person as a guidebook to help currently homeless people get back on their feet. This is just one example of the success of the Vancouver model, where success is marked by connecting drug users with others, with shared projects, and with a future filled with possibilities, rather than simply in terms of the cessation of drug use.

This model can be contrasted with the American model addressing the current opioid crisis. This model is better known as the war on drugs, or what many drug user activists call the war on people. They call it this because the American model of the war on drugs is primarily one characterised by the punishment and marginalisation of drug users and those associated with them. It has been a significant factor in the rise of mass incarceration in the country, and not unrelatedly, its policies have overwhelmingly impacted African-American and Latino-American communities in a negative manner. The war on drugs has also created a culture in which any person who problematically uses drugs is systematically dehumanised by being labeled an "addict," who almost by definition is considered to have lost all the capacities of what today's society considers a human to be, that is, rational and responsible. Because of this drug war "mentality," as many activists call it, too many drug users are further isolated as family, friends, and too often, medical and social service workers stigmatise and turn their backs on them. As if this were not enough, the war on drugs has absolutely failed to deter drug use, and this failure has cost American taxpayers over $50 billion annually. Not surprisingly, the current response in the United States to the opioid crisis has been a doubling down on the failed policies of this law and order approach.

For well over a generation, however, American drug user activists and their allies have worked hard to implement harm reduction policies despite the oppressive conditions of the war on drugs, and have been inspired by the Vancouver model to go beyond harm reduction's public health components. It is now time that Americans politicians and the medical establishment join them and begin to take the Vancouver model seriously as well. As a first step, this means the United States needs a robust harm reduction infrastructure—including safe consumption facilities— to address the public health aspects of the opioid crisis.

Ultimately, however, local projects of dynamic community-building are needed so that people can once again become connected with one another, engage in shared projects of purpose with others, find economic stability and security, and, thus, regain a future that matters to them. Only with such practices of attuned care will the United States finally begin to address the precarity, anxiety, and loneliness that truly lies at the heart of the opioid crisis.

4

From Opioids to Heroin: How Patients Make the Transition

Chris McGreal

Chris McGreal is the author of American Overdose *and a writer for the* Guardian. *He had previously worked as a correspondent for the newspaper in Washington, DC, Johannesburg, and Jerusalem.*

Florida is one of the states at the center of the opioid crisis, at one point leading the number of opioids prescribed by doctors by 90 percent. The state tried to remedy the issue by restricting access to opioids and shutting down pill mills. This helped decrease the number of deaths by opioid overdose but increased the number of people addicted to heroin, as those patients who lost access to prescription opioids turned to heroin to find their fix.

For James Fata, the transition from prescription painkillers to heroin was seamless.

The 24-year-old came to Florida to shake an addiction to opioid pills, but trying to go through rehab in a region known as the prescription capital of America proved too much. When a government crackdown curtailed his supply of pills, Fata turned to readily available heroin to fill the void.

"The pills were hard to get. They got to be very expensive. Heroin is cheap," said Fata, 24. "Almost everyone that I was close to, anybody that was doing pills with me, typically they would

"How cracking down on America's painkiller capital led to a heroin crisis," by Chris McGreal, Guardian News and Media Limited, May 25, 2016. Reprinted by permission.

at least get to the point where pills were not an option. You were either snorting heroin or shooting heroin."

Florida was the crucible of the opioid epidemic now gripping the US. Before deaths from opiates spiked nationwide, the state's south corridor earned the name "Oxy Express" for its liberal access to the extraordinarily powerful synthetic heroin painkiller, OxyContin.

But after Florida spent years trying to shake off its reputation by driving out of business the worst of the notorious "pill mills," the twist came that state officials hadn't predicted.

When the addicts Florida facilitated could not get prescription opioids any more, they turned to heroin.

"I'd like to say it's getting better because I see at least things are being brought to the surface and there's an advocacy movement," Fata said. "But on a numbers level, it's getting worse. On the amount of deaths I see, it's getting worse. The amount of heroin use I'm seeing, it's getting worse."

As heroin deaths in the US have more than tripled nationwide since 2010, critics say Florida's efforts to contain an epidemic unleashed within its borders have only had limited effect in curbing one crisis while making another worse.

Florida's problems started after OxyContin swept on to the market in 1996, just as medical authorities began pressing doctors to pay greater attention to alleviating pain. Unscrupulous businessmen in Florida spotted an opportunity.

Within a few years, hundreds of pain clinics popped up around the state dispensing opioid pills to just about anyone who asked. Among the earliest and biggest was American Pain in the Miami-Fort Lauderdale metro area, with a pharmacy run by former strippers and doctors carrying guns under their white coats.

It took in tens of millions of dollars a year selling OxyContin and generic versions containing oxycodone to people who travelled from Kentucky and West Virginia where painkillers were known as "hillbilly heroin." They came south along the "Oxy Express" by bus or the carload, sometimes driven by dealers who took a cut of the pills.

At one point, more than 90% of all the prescription opioids dispensed by doctors in the US were sold in Florida.

"Nothing Had Ever Brought Me to My Knees"

Robert Eaton was introduced to opioids at the age of 24 after suffering herniated discs in 2009. After a couple of months of therapy and low levels of painkillers, his doctor said he had done all he could for Eaton. The doctor pointed him to the pill mills.

"He recommended me to go see a pain management doctor. I started seeing him every month. Immediately he increased all of my prescriptions," he said.

Eaton reels off a list of hundreds of oxycodone, methadone and muscle relaxants he was prescribed each month.

"It's a lot but by the time I got to him, the pills already had a stranglehold on me. A lot more just seemed better. I didn't realise at the time just how far this thing was going to take me," he said. "Nothing had ever brought me to my knees. Once the pills went into my body, it was over. As soon I took that drug I was like, 'whoa, this is good. I need more of this now.'"

Those hooked on oxycodone say that they do not so much feel a craving for pills as a fear of not getting them and, as they put it, getting sick. If they don't get a fix, they get hit by increasingly intense pain from withdrawal much worse than the pain they were treating.

"By the end, I was locking myself in a room, never getting that kind of high," Eaton said. "Needing this to not get sick and to be able to get out of bed."

Eaton quickly came to realise that the doctor wasn't so much treating him as taking his money, writing a prescription, and getting him out of the door as fast as possible in order to get the next patient in.

"Not once did he ever ask me: 'Did your pain improve this month?' There was no intention to ever bring the medication level down at all. You're walking in and he's prescribing you the max," he said. "If you had insurance, it didn't matter. You paid cash to see the doctor."

Eaton is still not sure how much he spent between the doctors and the pills but said it ran into hundreds of dollars a day.

He lost his job as a Budweiser delivery driver because the pills affected his work. He lost his house. He even sold his stepchildren's toys.

"I would take the mortgage money. My wife at the time would try and scrounge up money to pay for things and I would steal it," he said.

Eaton found another job training as an emergency medic with a fire department and managed to keep his addiction hidden for a while.

"One day we walked into this lady's house. It was a grandma. She's sitting in her bed. She's dead and she had a pill bottle in her hand," he said. "That messed me up so bad I went and did roxies [oxycodone].

"My way to fix what I was experiencing was to go do the very drug that just killed her."

Oxycodone Down; Heroin Up

Florida started to crack down on "pill mills" in 2010.

American Pain was shut down in an FBI raid and its owners were imprisoned. The Florida legislature passed laws to kill off other pill mills and curtail the largely unfettered prescription of opioids. Deaths from oxycodone in Florida dropped 69% in the five years from 2010.

But the clampdown left those already addicted without a ready supply. It limited access to pills, forced up prices on the street, and made heroin a cheaper alternative. As the drug flooded in from Mexico, heroin deaths in Florida more than doubled in 2014 alone to a record 408.

Doctors also reported an increase in the number of babies born addicted to heroin, and Florida leads the US in new HIV-Aids infections, attributed to needle-sharing by drug users.

"What was going on here in Florida was different to any other place," Fata said. "The pill mills were blatantly illegal. Anybody could walk in and get a prescription. When that stopped, those people either latched on to people who still had a prescription or they moved to heroin. As those people they could latch on to dwindled and dwindled because it got stricter and more restrictive, the shift was to heroin."

The National Institute on Drug Abuse declared a heroin epidemic in south Florida two years ago.

The Journal of the American Medical Association Psychiatry noted a shift toward greater use by white people from affluent backgrounds and said that most were drawn to heroin after becoming addicted to opioid painkillers.

The 2014 study reported that 75% of those on heroin said they came to it via prescription opioids and noted a rise in heroin use as prescription opioid use decreased.

Florida officials were as caught off guard by the rise of heroin as they were by the sudden boom of the pill mills in the late 2000s.

Fata got hooked on prescription pills in his home state of Texas, where he grew up in what he describes as an upper-middle-class family. He began popping painkillers he found in his parents' cabinet when he was in his mid-teens, a pastime he said was common among his friends.

Before long he was hooked and taking even larger doses supplemented with heroin. He paid for his habit by dealing in drugs. But at the age of 20, after four years of drugs, his parents forced him to go to rehab in Florida.

"It got to a point where I was about to die and my parents said: 'You need to go to treatment," he said.

Fata was clean for about six months but, surrounded by people with easy access to prescriptions painkillers, his resolve failed.

"I was living in a halfway house when I relapsed. Working in a menial job. I just felt stuck. There was nowhere for me to go," he said.

But already the pills were becoming harder to find.

The federal authorities were moving against businessmen running Florida's pain clinics. Prosecutors called American Pain the US's largest illegal prescription drug ring, earning an estimated $43m in three years, and said it was responsible for at least 50 overdose deaths in Florida alone. Owner Jeff George was sent to prison for 20 years for the death of one of those patients. His brother Chris George received a reduced sentence of 14 years after testifying against doctors he hired.

The Florida legislature passed a package of reforms five years ago requiring that pain clinics be owned and run by a doctor. It also established a system to allow doctors and pharmacies to track prescriptions in an attempt to put an end to doctor shopping.

"I already knew that the scandal was shutting the pill mills down, so there's no way somebody like me, without a legitimate ailment, to get pills," Fata said.

Fata moved in with the man who would become his main supplier. His housemate had a prescription for back pain, still did a bit of doctor shopping, and sold some of the drugs. But it became more difficult as doctors became more wary with the Drug Enforcement Administration (DEA) and prosecutors sniffing around.

And the shortage drove the price of pills up on the black market.

"As soon as the prices of the pills went up, I knew I would just use heroin," Fata said. "I moved to heroin because the price of OxyContin turned to more expensive than the price per ounce of gold."

Heroin was about one-eighth of the price of pills for the same hit and more readily available.

With its rise has come an increase in deaths from a drug authorities say is as much as 50 times more powerful—fentanyl, a synthetic opiate frequently laced into heroin. The DEA last year issued a nationwide alert over what it called an alarming increase in the number of deaths related to fentanyl and heroin.

"New Addictions Every Day"

But the rise of heroin does not mean the prescription opioid crisis is going away.

Janet Colbert was instrumental in getting the pill mills closed down. Working as a neonatal intensive care nurse near Fort Lauderdale, Colbert had to deal with children born addicted to opioids through their mothers.

"In years past we had a cocaine baby once in a while. All of a sudden our unit is full of these babies. We're all like, what's going on? We had no idea why there were so many. Screaming. It was bad. You couldn't feed them. They're in withdrawal," she said.

"If there is a heroin epidemic, nine out of 10 heroin users start with prescription opiates. We'll never control the heroin if we don't control the opiates because there are new addictions every day."

Colbert points the finger at the drug manufacturers—led by Purdue Pharma, the maker of OxyContin—and a medical establishment she said that puts too much emphasis on prescribing powerful drugs to deal with pain.

In 2007, Purdue paid a $634m penalty for misrepresenting the drug's addictiveness. In December it reached a $24m settlement with Kentucky after the state claimed Purdue cost it "an entire generation" to OxyContin.

Colbert accuses the pharmaceutical companies and doctors of attempting to shift blame for the epidemic by accusing those hooked on prescription opioids of "abusing" the drugs.

That was the experience of Eaton, who calmly recalls the trauma of his years of addiction but becomes visibly angry when talking about drug manufacturers and doctors.

"This thing took me to a place where I didn't want to live any more, really. Do I have to accept responsibility? Yeah. I'm a drug addict. Am I a bad person? No. I was going to a doctor who was just taking my money from me. He wasn't trying to help me get better at all," he said. "I have a lot of friends who are dead who were getting prescriptions from doctors, and it's a doctor's job to protect them. It gets me really pissed off that they weren't protected."

Florida's attorney general, Pam Bondi, called doctors working in pill mills "drug dealers in white coats."

Some physicians have been called to account. A Lake Worth doctor, Sergio Rodriguez, was sentenced to 27 years in prison over more than four overdose deaths. But it has proved hard to convict others. Cynthia Cadet wrote more prescriptions than any other doctor at American Pain and was paid $1.5m. But a jury cleared her of criminal charges after she said she could not know if patients were lying about pain levels. She was later imprisoned for money laundering.

Colbert said that jailing a few doctors does not go far enough when hundreds were employed in what she regards as a criminal racket. She would like to see the state medical authorities strip them of their licences to practice.

Her organisation, Stopp Now, is also pushing for doctors to be required to use a monitoring programme that would tell them if a patient is obtaining prescriptions from another doctor. The programme is compulsory in 20 states but voluntary in Florida.

Colbert said state legislators have told her they will not support the measure because it is opposed by the Florida Medical Association.

"The doctors have a lot of clout and they don't want the legislation because somebody's telling them what to do," she said.

The Florida Medical Association did not respond to a request for comment.

Fata said he finally kicked heroin when he recognised it was going to kill him. He is studying to be a social worker and plans to return to Texas.

"I knew this past time, right before I got clean, that I was ready to kill myself," he said. "I was at breaking point."

Eaton also shook his reliance on drugs with the help of a religious group and now runs a personal training business. But getting off the pills came at a price. His marriage broke up. Friends were dying around him.

"My best friend died on just the prescriptions alone. His sister found him on the morning of his 30th birthday, dead in his room," he said.

Eaton missed the funeral because he was on the hunt for a fix.

5

Many of the Opioids Hitting the Streets Come from Criminal Labs in China

Kathleen McLaughlin

Kathleen McLaughlin is a science journalist who reports for Science *magazine and the* Guardian.

Illegal drug production in China presents a serious obstacle in various ways. On the one hand, American authorities are finding the fight against opioids and heroin a difficult one as more complex drugs are entering the market from China. On the other hand, Chinese authorities are struggling to crack down on illicit drugs as stricter drug regulations force the producers of illicit opiates deeper into the black market. To avoid regulations, crime labs change the compound of drugs like fentanyl by adding other substances that make the drug even more dangerous than it was before. This, in turn, worsens the opioid crisis.

Miller Atkinson was an addict from the very first time he shot up with heroin. "I fell in love with it. Everything else fell to the wayside," says the 24-year-old. "There was nothing that could have stopped me from getting high."

And that's what he did every day, for 9 months, in his family's upper middle class neighborhood in this Midwestern city. He dropped out of the University of Cincinnati. Like other users, he built up a tolerance to heroin and needed larger doses to find euphoria. Then, about 4 years ago, a powerful new combination hit the streets here: heroin cut with fentanyl, a synthetic opiate about 100 times more potent than morphine that's used to alleviate pain during and after surgery and in late-stage cancers. "It started trickling in, and we were like, 'Wow, that was good, we need to get more of that,'" he says. "It was more intense." So much so that friends who shot up with fentanyl-laced heroin started dying.

Atkinson was one of the lucky ones. After several misdemeanors and a felony heroin possession charge, he got his life back on track, and he is now studying for the law school entrance exam.

Fentanyl and its analogs are new faces of a worsening scourge. The United States consumes 85% of all the world's natural and synthetic opiates, which in 2015 factored in 33,091 U.S. deaths, up more than 4000 from the previous year, according to the U.S. Centers for Disease Control and Prevention. Opioid overdoses have quadrupled since 1999. When average U.S. life expectancies for men and women edged downward last year, for the first time in decades, many health professionals blamed opiate abuse.

The opium poppy is no longer the starting point for many of the opiates on the street. The new compounds, often sold mixed with heroin, originate in illicit labs in China. "For the cartels, why wait for a field of poppies to grow and harvest if you can get your hands on the precursor chemicals and cook a batch of fentanyl in a lab?" says Tim Reagan, resident agent in charge of the U.S. Drug Enforcement Administration's (DEA's) Cincinnati office.

DEA classified fentanyl as a schedule II drug decades ago, which makes it a felony to sell or use the opiate without a prescription. But in China, until recently, fentanyl was largely unregulated. In late 2015, the drug agency persuaded its Chinese counterpart to add 116 synthetic drugs to its list of controlled substances; fentanyl and several analogs were included. In response, underground Chinese labs began tweaking the fentanyl molecule, which is easy to alter for anyone with basic knowledge of chemistry and lab tools. By adding chemical groups, unscrupulous chemists have created new, unregulated variants, some of them even more potent than the original.

Public awareness of the crisis spiked last spring, after music icon Prince's death from an overdose of fentanyl. But in the months since then, the chemical one-upmanship has deepened the opiate crisis, as new and nastier substances appear on the streets in places like Cincinnati. The fentanyl derivatives not only allow makers and dealers to elude law enforcement; they blindside public health authorities and make addiction even riskier. "It's just going to get worse," Reagan says.

Last July, police and scientists here were bracing for a new villain—perhaps the deadliest fentanyl cousin yet. "We were hearing about something so dastardly we had to be prepared," recalls Lakshmi Sammarco, the coroner for Hamilton County, which includes Cincinnati. Carfentanil, an elephant tranquilizer that apparently had never been studied in humans, was showing up mixed into heroin in nearby cities and felling addicts. That month, a Canadian man was arrested in Calgary after authorities intercepted a 1-kilogram package of carfentanil labeled as "printer accessories," which he had ordered from China. Other synthetic opiates had found their way into Ohio via Canada, so it was only a matter of time before carfentanil would make the journey as well. "We all looked at each other and said, 'Alright, buckle your seat belts, this is going to get very bumpy,'" Sammarco says.

Fentanyl crosses the blood-brain barrier with ease. It binds to opioid receptors and floods the brain with dopamine, which creates intense euphoria but also slows the heart and depresses breathing. For most individuals, a lethal fentanyl dose is about 2 milligrams—an amount so minuscule that in a test tube it looks like a few grains of salt clinging to the glass. Carfentanil is 100 times stronger, making it about 10,000 times more potent than morphine. Crime labs keep autoinjectors of naloxone, the lifesaving opioid receptor antagonist, within reach in case their personnel are accidentally exposed to synthetic opiates.

Realizing what they were facing, Sammarco and her colleagues shifted into crisis mode, warning first responders that carfentanil overdoses could require double or triple doses of naloxone. They cautioned users not to dose up alone, and banned cops and emergency crews from testing drugs at crime scenes. (Last September, 11 police in Connecticut fell ill after accidentally inhaling fentanyl that was kicked up into the air during a drug bust.)

Then, the bomb went off. Over 6 days in late August 2016, Hamilton County saw 176 drug overdoses, primarily from carfentanil, the coroner's office says. After the initial shock wave, use of the drug ebbed—it was simply too powerful and dangerous for addicts and dealers looking to make a quick profit. "We get a little bit of breathing room," Sammarco says. "But we're always waiting for the other shoe to drop."

Hoping to stem the tide of synthetic opiates, DEA has taken the fight to China, as prolific a maker of illicit drugs as it is of legitimate chemicals. According to a U.S.-China Economic and Security Review Commission report last month, "China is a global source of illicit fentanyl and other [new psychoactive substances] because the country's vast chemical and pharmaceutical industries are weakly regulated and poorly monitored." In response to U.S. pressure, China has scheduled fentanyl and several other derivatives.

But enforcement is tough. Chinese labs producing the synthetic opiates play hide-and-seek with authorities. On their websites, they list fake addresses in derelict shopping centers or shuttered factories, and use third-party sales agents to conduct transactions that are hard to trace. The drugs themselves are easy to find with a Google search and to buy with a few mouse clicks. A recent check found more than a dozen Chinese sites advertising fentanyl, carfentanil, and other derivatives, often labeled as "research chemicals," for sale through direct mail shipments to the United States. On one website, carfentanil goes for $361 for 50 grams: tens of thousands of lethal doses.

The cat-and-mouse game extends to chemistry, as the makers tinker with fentanyl itself. Minor modifications like adding an oxygen atom or shifting a methyl group can be enough to create whole new entities that are no longer on the list of sanctioned compounds. Carfentanil itself was, until recently, unregulated in China.

The coroner's office in Cincinnati overflows with work. Lab analysts have set up shop in makeshift office spaces in the hallway. They are coping with a months-long case backlog created by the waves of new opiates washing into the region. In Hamilton County, as in many other jurisdictions, drug dealers can be charged with manslaughter when a customer overdoses and dies, but prosecutors can't charge a dealer without verifying what he sold. To confirm that victims have overdosed on illegal opiates and to support prosecution of drug dealers, Sammarco's team must parse the chemical composition of seized samples.

Other users can't help, as they generally "don't know what they're taking," says Tom Fallon, a lead investigator with the Hamilton County Heroin Task Force. A computer readout of one sample in the crime lab here illustrates why. The batch includes heroin, of course, but also caffeine, an antihistamine, an unidentified fentanyl compound, carfentanil, and another nasty analog, furanylfentanyl. Some recently seized batches have also been laced with ketamine, an anesthetic that has gained popularity in China as a recreational drug.

When the carfentanil wave struck, the county lab scrambled to prepare its analytical tools. One challenge was simply finding samples to compare to seized material. Veterinarians no longer use the substance, and commercial labs don't stock it. Eventually the coroner's office procured an expired batch from a nearby zoo. By October 2016, the county toxicology lab had fine-tuned its testing of blood and urine samples using a gas chromatograph mass spectrometer, which can find carfentanil at its smallest detectable dose. The machine shears mystery molecules into fragments, weighs them, and compares the pattern of masses to those from a known molecule. Like splitting Lego creations, breaking up the molecules produces the same pattern each time.

Another challenge with carfentanil is the dearth of literature on how much would cause a human to overdose or die, explains Bob Topmiller, Hamilton County's toxicologist. First responders and crime lab chemists are now building a body of research on its effects. "We're not a research lab," he says, "but there's a lot of information we've been able to obtain over the last several months that we've been able to share with other labs," such as molecular structures and toxicology reports.

Like other regions around the United States coping with a tide of mystery opiates, Hamilton County gets help identifying the compounds from DEA's own facilities, including the Special Testing and Research Laboratory, a plain building in an industrial development in Sterling, Virginia. In contrast to the Hamilton County coroner's office, the Sterling lab is brightly lit and uncluttered. Director Jeffrey Comparin and his team have at their disposal an arsenal of detection and chemical dissection tools for identifying unknown drugs. "It's not uncommon for us to build up a molecular model from scratch as we go," he says. A DEA chemist demonstrates by snapping a methyl group onto a plastic model of fentanyl.

China eventually banned methylfentanyl, driving down its production and pushing it deeper underground. Its crackdown on fentanyl and several analogs in 2015 led to a marked decline in those synthetic opiates in the United States, DEA says. And last month, after extensive negotiations with DEA, China added carfentanil and three more fentanyl analogs to its list of controlled substances.

Even before China scheduled carfentanil, the scourge had begun to fade in Ohio. Sammarco expects the final toll from that analog in Hamilton County last year, after all analyses are completed, will top 70 deaths. But a new threat has appeared. Traces of an unidentified fentanyl analog have cropped up in several batches from crime scenes. Hamilton County's scientists will search for a molecular match, add it to the list—and hope the new wave is less deadly than the last.

6

Despite What Many Believe, Doctors Are Not the Cause of the Opioid Crisis

Sally Satel

Sally Satel is a psychiatrist based in Washington, DC, who also works as a lecturer at the Yale University School of Medicine.

Doctors are not as responsible for the opioid crisis as many believe. It is very unlikely for patients who are being prescribed painkillers and have no prior history of addiction to become addicted to opioids. Based on research by the Cochrane Library, less than 1 percent of patients given a high dose of opioids become addicted to it. In this viewpoint, the author does not deny the rise in opioid prescriptions and opioid overdose cases, but wants to warn against attributing the crisis to careless handling of drug prescriptions.

A s an addiction psychiatrist, I have watched with serious concern as the opioid crisis has escalated in the United States over the past several years, and overdose deaths have skyrocketed. The latest numbers from the Centers for Disease Control and Prevention show fatalities spiraling up to about 42,000 in 2016, almost double the casualties in 2010 and more than five times the 1999 figures. The White House Council of Economic Advisers recently estimated that the opioid crisis cost the nation half a trillion dollars in 2015, based on deaths, criminal justice expenses and productivity losses. Meanwhile, foster care systems are overflowing

"The Myth of What's Driving the Opioid Crisis," by Sally Satel, Politico LLC, February 21, 2018. Reprinted by permission.

with children whose parents can't care for them, coroners' offices are overwhelmed with bodies and ambulance services are straining small-town budgets. American carnage, indeed.

I have also watched a false narrative about this crisis blossom into conventional wisdom: The myth that the epidemic is driven by patients becoming addicted to doctor-prescribed opioids, or painkillers like hydrocodone (e.g., Vicodin) and oxycodone (e.g., Percocet). One oft-quoted physician refers to opioid medication as "heroin pills." This myth is now a media staple and a plank in nationwide litigation against drugmakers. It has also prompted legislation, introduced last spring by Senators John McCain and Kirsten Gillibrand—the Opioid Addiction Prevention Act, which would impose prescriber limits because, as a news release stated, "Opioid addiction and abuse is commonly happening to those being treated for acute pain, such as a broken bone or wisdom tooth extraction."

But this narrative misconstrues the facts. The number of prescription opioids in circulation in the United States did increase markedly from the mid-1990s to 2011, and some people became addicted through those prescriptions. But I have studied multiple surveys and reviews of the data, which show that only a minority of people who are prescribed opioids for pain become addicted to them, and those who do become addicted and who die from painkiller overdoses tend to obtain these medications from sources other than their own physicians. Within the past several years, overdose deaths are overwhelmingly attributable not to prescription opioids but to illicit fentanyl and heroin. These "street opioids" have become the engine of the opioid crisis in its current, most lethal form.

If we are to devise sound solutions to this overdose epidemic, we must understand and acknowledge this truth about its nature.

For starters, among people who are prescribed opioids by doctors, the rate of addiction is low. According to a 2016 national survey conducted by the Substance Abuse and Mental Health Services Administration, 87.1 million U.S. adults used a prescription opioid—whether prescribed directly by a physician or obtained illegally—sometime during the previous year. Only 1.6 million of them, or about 2 percent, developed a "pain reliever use disorder," which includes behaviors ranging from overuse to overt addiction. Among patients with intractable, noncancer pain—for example, neurological disorders or musculoskeletal or inflammatory conditions—a review of international medical research by the Cochrane Library, a highly regarded database of systemic clinical reviews, found that treatment with long-term, high-dose opioids produced addiction rates of less than 1 percent. Another team found that abuse and addiction rates within 18 months after the start of treatment ranged from 0.12 percent to 6.1 percent in a database of half a million patients. A 2016 report in the *New England Journal of Medicine* concluded that in multiple published studies, rates of "carefully diagnosed" addiction to opioid medication averaged less than 8 percent. In a study several years ago, a research team purposely excluded chronic-pain patients with prior drug abuse and addiction from their data, and found that only 0.19 percent of the patients developed abuse and addiction to opioids.

Indeed, when patients do become addicted during the course of pain treatment with prescribed opioids, often they simultaneously face other medical problems such as depression, anxiety, other mental health conditions, or current or prior problems with drugs or alcohol. According to SAMHSA's 2014 National Survey on Drug Use and Health, more than three-fourths of those who misuse pain medication already had used other drugs, including benzodiazepines and inhalants, before they ever misused painkillers. And according to CDC data, at least half of all prescription opioid-related deaths are associated with other drugs, such as benzodiazepines, alcohol and cocaine; combinations that are often deadlier than the component drugs on their own. The physical and mental health issues that drive people to become addicted to drugs in the first place are very much part of America's opioid crisis and should not be discounted, but it is important to acknowledge the influence of other medical problems and other drugs.

Just because opioids in the medical context don't produce high rates of addiction doesn't mean doctors aren't overprescribing and doing serious harm. The amount of opioids prescribed per person in 2016, though a bit lower than the previous year, was still considered high by the CDC—more than three times the amount of opioids dispensed in 1999. Some doctors routinely give a month's supply of opioids for short-term discomfort when only a few days' worth or even none at all is needed. Research suggests that patients given post-operation opioids don't end up needing to use most of their prescribed dose.

In turn, millions of unused pills end up being scavenged from medicine chests, sold or given away by patients themselves, accumulated by dealers and then sold to new users for about $1 per milligram. As more prescribed pills are diverted, opportunities arise for nonpatients to obtain them, abuse them, get addicted to them and die. According to SAMHSA, among people who misused prescription pain relievers in 2013 and 2014, about half said that they obtained those pain relievers from a friend or relative, while only 22 percent said they received the drugs from their doctor. The rest either stole or bought pills from someone they knew, bought from a dealer or "doctor-shopped" (i.e., obtained multiple prescriptions from multiple doctors). So diversion is a serious problem, and most people who abuse or become addicted to opioid pain relievers are not the unwitting pain patients to whom they were prescribed.

While reining in excessive opioid prescriptions should help limit diversion and, in theory, suppress abuse and addiction among those who consume the diverted supply, it will not be enough to reduce opioid deaths today. In the first decade of the 2000s, the opioid crisis almost seemed to make sense: The volume of prescribed opioids rose in parallel with both prescription overdose deaths and treatment admissions for addiction to prescription opioids. Furthermore, 75 percent of heroin users applying to treatment programs initiated their opioid addiction with pills, so painkillers were seen as the "gateway" to cheap, abundant heroin after their doctors finally cut them off. ("Ask your doctor how prescription pills can lead to heroin abuse," blared massive billboards from the Partnership for a Drug-Free New Jersey.) If physicians were more restrained in their prescribing, the logic went, fewer of their patients would become addicted, and the pipeline to painkiller addiction and ultimately to heroin would run dry.

It's not turning out that way. While the volume of prescriptions has trended down since 2011, total opioid-related deaths have risen. The drivers for the past few years are heroin and, mostly, fentanyl, a synthetic opioid that is 50 times as potent as heroin. Fentanyl has legitimate medical use, but there is also illicit fentanyl, trafficked mostly from China, often via the Dark Web. Fentanyl and heroin (which itself is usually tainted to some extent with the fentanyl) together were present in more than two-thirds of all opioid-related deaths in 2016, according to CDC data. Painkillers were present in a little more than one-third of opioid-related deaths, but a third of those painkiller deaths also included heroin or fentanyl. While deaths from prescription opioids have basically leveled off, when you look at deaths in which prescription opioids *plus* heroin and fentanyl were present, then the recorded deaths attributed to prescription opioids continue to climb, too. (An especially pernicious element in the mix is counterfeiters with pill presses who sell illicit fentanyl in pill form deceptively labeled as OxyContin and other opioid pain relievers or benzodiazepines.)

Notably, more current heroin users these days seem to be initiating their opioid trajectory with heroin itself—an estimated 33 percent as of 2015—rather than with opioid painkillers. In the first decade of the 2000s, about 75 to 80 percent of heroin users started using opioids with pills (though not necessarily pain medication prescribed by a doctor for that particular person). It seems that, far more than prescribed opioids, the unpredictability of heroin and the turbocharged lethality of fentanyl have been a prescription for an overdose disaster.

Intense Efforts to Curb Prescribing Are Under Way

Pharmacy benefit managers, such as CVS, insurers and health care systems have set limits or reduction goals. State-based prescription drug monitoring programs help doctors and pharmacists identify patients who doctor-shop, ER hop or commit insurance fraud. As of July, 23 states had enacted legislation with some type of limit, guidance or requirement related to opioid prescribing. McCain and Gillibrand's federal initiative goes even further, to impose a blanket ban on refills of the seven-day allotment for acute pain. And watchdog entities such as the National Committee for Quality Assurance have endorsed a system that compares the number of patients receiving over a certain dose of opioids with the performance rating for a physician.

A climate of precaution is appropriate, but not if it becomes so chilly that doctors fear prescribing. This summer, a 66-year-old retired orthopedic surgeon who practiced in Northern California— I'll call her Dr. R—contacted me. For more than 30 years, she had been on methadone, a legitimate opioid pain medication, for an excruciating inflammatory bladder condition called interstitial cystitis. With the methadone, she could function as a surgeon. "It gave me a life. I would not be here today without it," she told me. But one day in July, her doctor said the methadone had to stop. "She seemed to be worried that she was doing something illegal," Dr. R told me.

Dr. R was fortunate. She found another doctor to prescribe methadone. But her experience of nonconsensual withdrawal of opioids is not isolated. Last year, the nonprofit Pain News Network conducted an online survey among 3,100 chronic pain patients who had found relief with opioids and had discussed this in online forums. While not necessarily a representative sample of all individuals with chronic pain who are on opioids, the survey was informative: 71 percent of respondents said they are no longer prescribed opioid medication by a doctor or are getting a lower dose; 8 out of 10 said their pain and quality of life are worse; and more than 40 percent said they considered suicide as a way to end their pain. The survey was purposely conducted a few months after the CDC released guidelines that many doctors, as well as insurance carriers and state legislatures, have erroneously interpreted as a government mandate to discontinue opioids. In other accounts, patients complain of being interrogated by pharmacists about their doses; sometimes they are even turned away.

The most tragic consequence is suicide. Thomas F. Kline, an internist in Raleigh, North Carolina, has chronicled 23 of them. His count is surely a harbinger of further patient abandonment to come. Meanwhile, so-called pain refugees—chronic pain patients whose doctors have dropped them—search out physicians to treat them, sometimes traveling more than a hundred miles or relocating. And in a recent Medscape survey, half the doctors who were polled expressed fear of violent reactions if patients were refused the prescription.

Knowing all this, what should we do about the opioid crisis? First, we must be realistic about who is getting in trouble with opioid pain medications. Contrary to popular belief, it is rarely the people for whom they are prescribed. Most lives do not come undone, let alone end in overdose, after analgesia for a broken leg or a trip to the dentist. There is a subset of patients who are vulnerable to abusing their medication—those with substance use histories or with mental health problems. Ideally, they should inform physicians of their history, and, in turn, their doctors should elicit such information from them.

Still, given that diverted pills, not prescribed medication taken by patients for pain, are the greater culprit, we cannot rely on doctors or pill control policies alone to be able to fix the opioid crisis. What we need is a demand-side policy. Interventions that seek to reduce the *desire* to use drugs, be they painkillers or illicit opioids, deserve vastly more political will and federal funding than they have received. Two of the most necessary steps, in my view, are making better use of anti-addiction medications and building a better addiction treatment infrastructure.

Methadone and buprenorphine are opioid medications for treating addiction that can be prescribed by doctors as a way to wean patients off opioids or to maintain them stably. These medications have been shown to reduce deaths from all causes, including overdose. A third medication, naltrexone, blocks opioids' effect on the brain, and prevents a patient who tries heroin again from experiencing any effects. In 2016, however, only 41.2 percent of the nation's treatment facilities offered at least one form of medication, and 2.7 percent offered all three medications, according to a recent review of a national directory published by SAMHSA. We must move beyond the outmoded thinking and inertia that keep clinics from offering these medications.

Motivated patients also benefit greatly from cognitive behavioral therapy and from the hard work of recovery—healing family rifts, reintegrating into the workforce, creating healthy social connections, finding new modes of fulfillment. This is why treatment centers that offer an array of services, including medical care, family counseling and social services, have a better shot at promoting recovery. That treatment infrastructure must be fortified. The Excellence in Mental Health Act of 2014, a Medicaid-funded project, established more robust health centers in eight states. In 2017, House and Senate bills were introduced to expand the project to 11 more. It's a promising effort that could be a path to public or private insurance-based community services and an opportunity to set much-needed national practice standards.

These two priorities are among the 56 recommendations put forth last October by President Donald Trump's Commission on Combating Drug Addiction and the Opioid Crisis. Indeed, there is no dearth of ideas. In Congress, more than 90 bills aimed at the opioid crisis have been introduced in the 115th session, dozens of hearings have been held and later this month, the House Energy and Commerce Committee will begin holding a week of legislative hearings on measures to fight the opioid crisis. The White House's 2019 budget seeks $13 billion over two years for the opioid epidemic, and the president recently nominated a "drug czar" to helm the Office of Drug Control Policy, though the candidate has minimal experience in the area.

As we sort through and further pursue these policies, we need to make good use of what we know about the role that prescription opioids plays in the larger crisis: that the dominant narrative about pain treatment being a major pathway to addiction is wrong, and that an agenda heavily weighted toward pill control is not enough.

7

Opioids Cannot Be the Ultimate Solution in Pain Treatment

Timothy J. Atkinson, Jennifer H. Scruggs, and Tracey L. Perkins

Atkinson, Scruggs, and Perkins are health care professionals who focus on pain management at the VA Tennessee Valley Healthcare System.

One major contributor to the opioid crisis is health care providers' lack of understanding of how to treat pain. Only approximately 3 percent of medical schools provide pain management training to their students. Therefore, even though treating pain has become essential for doctors, they struggle to find ways to treat their patients (especially noncancer patients suffering from chronic pain), relying too heavily on opioids as a solution. Undertreated pain has indeed been a vital problem in the past, but opioids might not be the way to resolve it.

O piates have been available, in one form or another, for thousands of years. While varied recreational, spiritual, and medicinal uses have continued over time, the drug's mode, delivery, and function have been modernized.

In the past 30 years, the therapeutic use of opioids has undergone several major shifts. The 1980s were characterized by fear of opioids and addiction even among patients being treated for cancer, which resulted in concern for the undertreatment of pain.

"Where Did the War on Pain Go Wrong?" by Timothy J. Atkinson, Jennifer H. Scruggs and Tracey L. Perkins, Practical Pain Management, Vertical Health LLC, September 6, 2016. Reprinted by permission.

In turn, a low risk of addiction in cancer patients was used to justify prescription opioids for chronic noncancer pain.[1] Throughout the 1990s, support for opioid use for chronic pain grew among pain specialists, professional societies, and various organizations until opioids for chronic noncancer pain became the standard of care.

The Federation of State Medical Boards endorsed the move in 1998 in its model guidelines, which were updated in 2004.[2] Substantial increases in opioid prescriptions were also fueled by the Joint Commission requirement for pain to be assessed as a vital sign in every encounter—the fifth vital sign.[3]

From 1999 to 2010, prescriptions for opioids increased by 400% and, unfortunately, this trend was accompanied by a corresponding increase in prescription opioid overdose deaths.[4,5] The increase in deaths associated with opioid abuse and misuse could, in part, be considered the unintentional result of a sincere intent to treat pain.

Chronic opioid therapy has now become a political target and a treatment dilemma for clinicians and patients alike. Overprescribing and overreliance on opioid therapy are key concerns, but the root causes are multifactorial. Many attribute the current crisis to the aggressive marketing of newer extended-release opioid formulations. While expectations that the formulations would reduce misuse and abuse ultimately proved false, such marketing campaigns may continue to influence and misinform physicians in the absence of dedicated evidence-based pain education and core competencies.

Professional education, or lack thereof, is another factor. Currently, less than 3% of medical schools incorporate pain management into their curriculum, yet chronic pain is the most common reason patients see a provider, and it accounts for 40% of all visits in primary care.[6] In a survey of primary care providers, 73% expressed frustration with treating chronic pain patients, and 38% were dissatisfied with their ability to treat pain.[7] Limited time for patient encounters and provider frustration can easily lead to increasing prescriptions for opioids or refusal to treat pain due to fear of regulatory reprisals or mistreatment. With

40 million Americans living with moderate to severe pain daily, and an aging population, an investment in education and training will be required to meet the demands of current clinical practice.[8]

The Institute of Medicine's 2011 report "Relieving Pain in America" reminds us that despite over a decade of focusing on its treatment, pain remains a significant public health burden ($635 billion annually) that warrants a cultural transformation in prevention, care, education, and research.[9]Among the National Institutes of Health's recommendations in its National Pain Strategy, released in March 2016, is that "chronic pain is a biopsychosocial condition that often requires integrated, multimodal, and interdisciplinary treatment, all components of which should be evidence-based."[10] Both reports endorse interdisciplinary and multimodal approaches to pain management that, despite the highest level of evidence supporting improved outcomes, have all but disappeared in the US outside of integrative health systems due to lack of reimbursement by managed care organizations.[11,12] Similarly, reimbursement for evidence-based therapies like cognitive behavioral therapy, acupuncture, chiropractic, massage, and physical therapy are often not covered, decreasing pain patients' access to tools proven to reduce reliance on opioid therapy while improving functional outcomes.[13] It doesn't seem surprising then that prescription opioids have increased dramatically, since alternatives to pain medications and procedures are limited.

Several assumptions borrowed from cancer pain have had a negative impact on chronic noncancer pain management. The risk of addiction in chronic pain patients was underestimated because duration of cancer pain, diagnosis, and treatment does not correlate with the length of exposure in chronic pain patients. Long-term exposure to opioid medications, in particular, increases the risk of opioid use disorder.[14] However, in patients with no personal or family history of addiction, no systematic review has shown a risk of addiction greater than 3.27% in the chronic pain population.[15]

In addition, the undertreatment of pain has led to the accepted adage, "Pain is whatever the patient says it is," which encourages assessment and treatment of pain but often is misinterpreted as justification for opioid therapy without appropriate diagnosis or pathology. Even in the treatment of cancer pain, a diagnosis identifying a potential cause of severe pain is necessary to receive any medication therapy, including opioids. Similarly, the concept that opioids have no "ceiling effect" has led to high-dose opioid therapy limited only by side effects, and has resulted in an ever-growing body of evidence showing that long-term side effects like sleep apnea and hypogonadism are dose-dependent.

Perhaps opioids will always be synonymous with pain management, but we got here by allowing opioids to become a central treatment focus without considering other medications and treatment modalities.

References

1. Porter J, Jick H. Addiction rare in patients treated with narcotics. *N Engl J Med.* 1980;302(2):123.

2. Federation of State Medical Boards of the United States Inc. Model policy for the use of controlled substances for the treatment of pain. *J Pain Palliat Care Pharmacother.* 2005;19(2):73-78.

3. Phillips DM. JCAHO pain management standards are unveiled. Joint Commission on Accreditation of Healthcare Organizations. *JAMA.* 2000;284(4):428-429.

4. Frenk SM, Porter KS, Paulozzi LJ. *Prescription Opioid Analgesic Use Among Adults: United States, 1999–2012.* NCHS data brief, no 189. Hyattsville, MD: National Center for Health Statistics; 2015.

5. Jones C, Mack K, Paulozzi L. Pharmaceutical overdose deaths, United States, 2010. *JAMA.* 2013;309(7):657-659.

6. Vadivelu N, Mitra S, Hines R, Elia M, Rosenquist R. Acute pain in undergraduate medical education: an unfinished chapter! *Pain Pract.* 2012;12(8):663-671.

7. Dobscha S, Corson K, Flores J, Tansill E, Gerrity M. Veterans affairs primary care clinicians' attitudes toward chronic pain and correlates of opioid prescribing rates. *Pain Med.* 2008;9(5):564-571.

8. Nahin RL. Estimates of pain prevalence and severity in adults: United States, 2012. *J Pain.* 2015;16(8):769-780.

9. Institute of Medicine. *Relieving Pain in America: A Blueprint for Transforming Prevention, Care, Education, and Research.* NIH National Academy of Sciences. June 29, 2011. Available at: http://www.ncbi.nlm.nih.gov/pubmed/22553896. Accessed July 4, 2016.

10. National Institutes of Health. *National Pain Strategy*. March 18, 2016. Available at: https://iprcc.nih.gov/docs/DraftHHSNationalPainStrategy.pdf. Accessed July 4, 2016.

11. Turk D, Stanos S, Palermo T, et al. *Interdisciplinary Pain Management*. Glenview, IL: American Pain Society; 2010.

12. Schatman ME. Interdisciplinary chronic pain management: international perspectives. *Pain Clin Updates*. 2012;20(7):1-5.

13. American Academy of Pain Medicine (AAPM). Position statement: minimum insurance benefits for patients with chronic pain. December 2011. Available at: http://www.painmed.org/files/minimum-insurance-benefits-for-patients-with-chronic-pain.pdf. Accessed July 3, 2016.

14. Edlund M, Martin B, Russo J, et al. The role of opioid prescription in incident opioid abuse and dependence among individuals with chronic non-cancer pain: the role of opioid prescription. *Clin J Pain*. 2014;30(7):557-564.

15. Fishbain D, Cole B, Lewis J, et al. What percentage of chronic nonmalignant pain patients exposed to chronic opioid analgesic therapy develop abuse/addiction and/or aberrant drug-related behaviors? A structured evidence-based review. *Pain Med*. 2008;9(4):444-459.

8

As Cases of Opioid Addiction Increase, So Do Cases of Sex Trafficking

Kristin Detrow

Kristin Detrow is a freelance writer based in Maryland who works with sexual assault and human trafficking victims at the Shenandoah Women's Center in West Virginia.

Sometimes when those addicted to drugs have nothing else to steal or sell in exchange for drugs, they traffic family members. These victims are often women and girls, though men and boys can also be victims. Unfortunately, most of these victims of sex trafficking are filed under prostitution in the legal system, but when carefully examining how sex workers entered this world and how they struggle to leave it, it becomes clear that quite often they did not consent to it. These examples of trafficking in West Virginia offer a key example of how the opioid epidemic is adding to cases of sex trafficking.

January is "Human Trafficking Awareness" month, but for many Americans the term is likely to call to mind Hollywood scenarios, with Albanian Mafiosos kidnapping fresh-faced college students, vile foreign millionaires in the shadows bidding on scantily clad girls quaking on auction blocks, while a hero (Liam Neeson, maybe) is prowling in the background, hell-bent on rescue and vengeance.

"The Link Between Opioid Abuse and Sex Trafficking," by Kristin Detrow, January 17, 2018. This article originally appeared in The Crime Report (www.thecrimereport.org).

Actually, the trafficking problem is much closer to home. The Hollywood scripts make great movies, but they are a far cry from what trafficking victims actually experience, and they sidestep what amounts to an epidemic in human trafficking that is playing out in communities across America.

A case in point is West Virginia's eastern panhandle, where the Shenandoah Women's Center has been operating for over 30 years to provide services to victims of sexual assault, domestic violence, LGBT targeting, and trafficking.

In our state, which leads the nation in poverty and drug overdoses, trafficking frequently looks more like this: A drug-addicted parent loses his or her job and other supports, and spirals downward into addiction. With nothing left to sell or steal, the addict decides to sell their partner—or their child—for drugs or money.

"Anne" is a classic example of how the opioid crisis in West Virginia has fueled human trafficking. Anne was a 25-year-old white woman with no kids, living in the urban Martinsburg area. She had a history of childhood trauma and no stable family ties. After Anne's boyfriend started using heroin, she soon became addicted as well. A few years into their relationship he told her that she would need to start sleeping with some of his friends and drug connections.

Although Anne didn't want to, she did it. About a year into the arrangement, she encountered some violent johns who wanted her to perform sex acts she wasn't comfortable with. Anne told her boyfriend that she wanted to stop. It was at that point that he threatened her life. Finally, after a brutal rape, she called our hotline and entered our shelter.

Anne was one of the first victims our agency labeled as being trafficked by an intimate partner. Although we had been serving victims like her for years, we hadn't been identifying them as trafficking victims. Anne said that many of her friends on the street had similar stories, and in fact, referred a number of women to us over the years.

Identifying victims of inter-familial trafficking can be difficult. Children often are unaware that money has exchanged hands. It is common for perpetrators to go through a grooming process with young teens who may feel that this person is their "boyfriend." Meanwhile, the individual is not aware that he or she has been bought for sex.

Crittenton Services is a trauma-focused residential treatment facility serving girls in ages 12-18 in West Virginia. In a Jan. 3 interview, Laura Smith, clinical therapist at Crittenton Services told NPR's *Morning Edition* that at least nine of the 30 girls living in the facility at that time reported they were sexually trafficked by a family member.

"So in those cases, they don't understand mom or dad is getting money on the side from that relationship, too," Smith said. "That part is kind of hidden, usually when the girls feel like they're in a relationship with those individuals."

Intimate partners such as wives or girlfriends are sometimes viewed by the legal system and those "outside" of the situation as prostitutes or, perhaps, as victims of domestic violence.

But under the definition of trafficking as the "use of fraud, force or coercion" to obtain labor or commercial sex, they have been trafficked. Additionally, while the vast majority of trafficking victims are female, boys and men are not immune.

Our program serves the three counties in the Eastern Panhandle of West Virginia, home to both rural and DC Metro areas. Berkeley County is split down the middle by Interstate 81. Easy travel via the Interstate, close proximity to large cities, the desperation of living in an extremely rural and impoverished state all make our region susceptible to both trafficking and opioid abuse.

According to Shared Hope International, 90 percent of prostitutes and those working in the commercial sex industry are controlled by a pimp or a trafficker. That staggering statistic should give us all pause.

We see them every day: Young girls and women walking the streets of downtown Martinsburg, near the 7-Eleven. Hanging out at the hotels on Winchester Avenue where most of us wouldn't even pull in to do a U-turn in broad daylight.

What if, instead of a fleeting moment of pity and revulsion, we thought of these people as victims? Are they drug addicts? Probably. Addiction has been an issue with at least half, if not more, of the trafficking victims we serve at the Shenandoah Women's Center. It is much easier for a trafficker to control an addict.

"You can make someone do just about anything when they are dope sick," according to Katie Spriggs, executive director of the Shenandoah Center.

Consider this. The average age a victim enters "the life" of prostitution is between 12 and 14. Traffickers are experts in selecting victims who are vulnerable and even have their own glossary of terms to refer to both perpetrators and victims.

For example, a "Romeo Pimp" prides himself on his ability to control his girls primarily through psychological manipulation. These pimps often shower their victims with expensive gifts, dates, and affection while recruiting them, but extreme violence is a constant threat.

In 2016, Carlos Curtis, currently serving a life sentence for trafficking a 12-year-old girl, spoke to a *Baltimore Sun* reporter about the grooming process.

"Why does a prostitute need a pimp?" Curtis said. "To guide her, to love her, to protect her. The pimp is her father that she never had. He is that big brother that she misses, or the boyfriend from back in the day…

"He is the popular guy in school that never paid her attention in class. To her, he is what Christ is to a Christian… The blood that pumps in her heart and keeps her legs moving. Without him, there's no her."

The term "Guerilla Pimp" refers to a pimp who uses physical violence and force to control his victims. If a girl is resistant to being "turned out," she may be put through the "seasoning" process. This includes psychological abuse; gang rape; beatings; sodomy;

deprivation of food, water and sleep; holding her children hostage; or threatening loved ones.

Seasoning is a pimp's way of breaking victims and ensuring their compliance. When a vulnerable girl realizes what she has gotten into, it is often too late for her to escape safely, or the feelings she has for her trafficker, similar to those of victims of domestic abuse, keep her tethered to him by a sick sense of loyalty and gratefulness.

To date, the Shenandoah Women's Center has served an estimated 150 victims since 2012.

"As we have done our research, trained our staff, and done outreach, our numbers are rising exponentially. We realize now that we have been serving trafficking victims all along, but they were not labeled as such," Spriggs said.

"We have no way of knowing how many we are missing. I think the problem is much bigger than anyone realizes."

What can the average person do to help? At the Shenandoah Women's Center, advocates are trained to recognize and serve victims of Human Trafficking. We conduct outreach to truck stops and hotels. We partner with local medical providers as well as interested persons in the community to enable them to recognize a victim when they encounter one. We provide medical and legal advocacy, counseling services, an emergency shelter, and a 24-hour victim hotline for victims all at no cost.

We also reach into schools to talk to kids about this issue in hopes of preventing students from becoming victims, and to enable teachers and counselors to spot at-risk children.

Rebecca Bender, a survivor and nationally recognized expert on domestic Human Trafficking, says that it is time to stop glamorizing prostitution and the sex industry. Lured away from her Oregon home with her young daughter by her trafficker, whom she thought was her boyfriend, she was trafficked in Las Vegas and traded between three pimps for six years before escaping.

"Those who bought me were usually in denial. They wanted to believe I was working my way through school and that I was, in fact, that independent 'happy hooker,'" Bender said. "They'd say things like, 'You're putting yourself through college, right?' As if they were grasping at any last justification of their own conscience."

On her website, Bender said the day of reckoning is on the way.

"It will be here sooner if the truth about prostitution were known," she writes. "If men and women would stand up and start changing the way our culture glamorizes and normalizes 'prostitution.'"

Each of us can do something.

Educate yourself on this crisis. Have compassion when you see someone you think could be a victim. Teach your sons to respect women, and most importantly, hold your daughters close and show them how special they are.

Step into the life of an at-risk young person in your circle.

You could be the one who prevents him or her from falling prey to a modern-day slave owner.

9

Analyzing How the Opioid Crisis Affects Different Groups Can Lead to Its Solution

Paola Scommegna

Paola Scommegna is a senior writer at the Population Reference Bureau. She covers academic research on health, wellness, and aging for program planners and lawmakers.

Even though the opioid crisis can affect anyone regardless of education level, it has done the most damage among less-educated Americans, especially non-Hispanic whites. Not only are less-educated people more susceptible to depression and drug addiction, they are more likely to find themselves in dangerous jobs that put them at risk of injury. This in turn can lead to use of painkillers and potential addiction to opioids. Moreover, this epidemic saw a rise in overdose cases among blacks and women. In this viewpoint, Scommegna argues that to fix this crisis, we must understand the people most affected by it.

The prescription opioid painkillers that helped fuel the surge in U.S. drug overdose deaths were first approved by the Federal Drug Administration in late 1995.

The before-and-after fatality rates tell a shocking story: In 1994, the age-adjusted drug overdose death rate was 4.8 deaths per 100,000 people; by 2015, the rate had more than tripled to

Paola Scommegna, "Opioid Overdose Epidemic Hits Hardest for The Least Educated," Population Reference Bureau, January 10, 2018. Accessed at www.prb.org. Reprinted by permission. All rights reserved.

16.3 per 100,000. [1] Since then, the overdose death rate has continued to climb. Provisional estimates for 2016 suggest it reached 19.8 deaths per 100,000, more than quadrupling since 1994. [2] While prescription opioids fueled the initial surge in overdose deaths after 1995, heroin and fentanyl-type compounds—which tend to be illicitly produced—are the main drivers now.

"Intense attention and action" is what experts at the U.S. Centers for Disease Control and Prevention (CDC) argue is needed to counter the epidemic.

Key to any response is an understanding of the people and places hardest hit, says Jessica Ho of the University of Southern California.

Shannon Monnat of Syracuse University agrees. "Overdose deaths are not randomly distributed across the country."

These researchers point out that the steep rise in fatal overdoses is unusual and unanticipated, occurring at the same time that death rates from heart disease, cancer, and injury-related causes have declined.

The only other comparable surges in deaths in high-income countries are alcohol-related deaths in the former Soviet Union and the HIV/AIDS epidemic in Europe and North America, Ho reports.

Higher Toll Among the Least Educated

The U.S. opioid epidemic has taken the lives of rising numbers of people with all levels of education. However, deaths have grown increasingly more concentrated among those with lower levels of education, particularly among non-Hispanic whites.

More-educated adults in the United States tend to live longer than less-educated individuals. The differences increase in a stair-step pattern by education level, with the widest difference between college graduates and those without high school degrees. This gap has widened over the past two decades, resulting in part from steep increases in drug overdose deaths among those without college degrees, reports Ho in an article published in the journal *Demography*. [3]

Ho analyzed life expectancy differences by education level, using data for 1992 through 2011 from the National Health Interview Survey combined with data from the National Vital Statistics System. She focused on adults ages 30 to 60—the prime working years—because this age group is disproportionately affected by the overdose epidemic.

Her analysis shows that between 1992 and 2011 drug overdose deaths represented a sizable share of the widening difference in life expectancy among college graduates and those with less education. For example, among non-Hispanic whites, opioid deaths account for 99 percent of the *growth* in the life expectancy gap between men with college degrees and those without high school diplomas; among women, opioid deaths could be blamed for 42 percent of the growth in the life expectancy gap between the two education groups.

Ho argues that people with low education levels often experience limited job opportunities and poor economic prospects, leaving them vulnerable to depression, despair, and drug addiction. Among the Interrelated reasons for this:

- Less-educated individuals tend to work in settings that "increase their risk of workplace injuries, disability, and chronic health conditions, which lead to a greater likelihood of being prescribed opioid painkillers," raising their risk of addiction.
- People with low education levels are more concentrated in rural areas, where the emergency medical response for overdose victims may be more limited.
- Less-educated individuals who also have limited incomes may have greater financial incentives to participate in schemes that involve reselling opioids (such as seeking prescriptions from multiple doctors), which also increase their access to these drugs and the likelihood of addiction.
- Compared with more-educated people, less-educated people "may have fewer resources to combat drug addiction,

including financial resources, access to scarce slots in drug treatment programs, and support from social networks."

Strategies to address the opioid crisis should consider the economic constraints and treatment barriers that people with low education levels may face, she argues.

Women's Overdose Rates Rising Closer to Men's

Historically, men have had higher drug overdose rates than women, but the difference is narrowing slightly with the current epidemic. In the *Demography* study described above, Ho sees a "gender convergence," with women's overdose death rates increasing more rapidly than men's and rising closer to their levels.

Her analysis of overdose death rates over time shows that men without college degrees would have been better off in 2011 if their drug overdose rates dropped to the 2011 levels observed for college-educated men, rather than if their rates returned to pre-epidemic levels for men without college degrees. These results suggest that mortality differences by education remain "fairly sharp" for men. But for women, Ho shows that high school graduates and those with some college would have been better off in 2011 if their overdose rates dropped back to the level their own education group had in the early 1990s, indicating that these two groups of women experienced large increases in overdose deaths.

One reason women's overdose rates have risen so rapidly recently may be that women tend to be more connected to the health care system and visit health care providers more often than men. They thus may be prescribed prescription painkillers at higher rates, Ho suggests. Evidence shows that compared with men, women may become addicted more quickly and have greater difficulty quitting, she reports.

Opioid Death Rates Increasing Among Blacks

In analysis that focuses exclusively on opioid-related drug fatalities, researchers' preliminary findings show that between 2010 and

2015 mortality rates increased faster for blacks than whites. [4] Monica Alexander and Magali Barbieri of the University of California, Berkeley; and Mathew Kiang of Harvard University examine vital statistics data on opioid-related deaths by race between 2000 and 2015, demonstrating that the opioid epidemic is not "white only."

For 2015, they calculate that the opioid-related overdose mortality rate for whites was 12.2 per 100,000, nearly twice the rate for blacks (about 6.6 per 100,000). However, between 2000 and 2015, the opioid death rate increased 51 percent among whites but 87 percent among blacks.

To understand these dynamics, Alexander, Barbieri, and Kiang examine two different time periods and different types of opioids. Between 2000 and 2010, whites experienced much larger increases in opioid overdose deaths than blacks, mainly due to a rise in fatalities from prescription opioid painkillers. But between 2010 and 2015, both blacks and whites experienced sizeable increases in their opioid overdose death rate. This increase is mainly related to a rise in deaths from illicit opioids—heroin and highly potent fentanyl-type compounds.

In addition, the researchers find that deaths related to heroin and fentanyl-type drugs increase with age among blacks, but are more concentrated among younger whites.

They note that after 2010 the prescription painkiller OxyContin was reformulated to be less addictive, and distribution restrictions at the national and state levels began. These changes may have contributed to a greater demand for heroin, leading to a growing supply and falling prices. More lethal types of heroin laced with fentanyl also became more widely available after 2010.

Because increases in overdose death rates show no sign of slowing, Alexander, Barbieri, and Kiang argue that policymakers aiming to improve health policy and rehabilitation programs should consider how different racial groups tend to abuse different drug types.

Economic Distress, Job Loss Key

Drug overdose deaths are not evenly spread across the country, as ongoing research that also examines deaths from suicide and alcohol shows. Just as people with specific characteristics face higher risks, certain places are "shouldering a much heavier burden" than others, reports Shannon Monnat. [5]

She shows that rural (nonmetropolitan) and small urban counties that have high concentrations of deaths from drug overdose, suicide, and alcohol abuse also tend to feature:

- Large shares of economically vulnerable residents—based on a composite index that includes poverty, unemployment, disability, households headed by single parents, lack of health insurance, and public assistance receipt.
- Declines in median household income since 1980 stemming from job losses in manufacturing and natural resources.

In Monnat's view, interventions should target communities with populations in "significant economic distress," focusing on "places that have experienced major labor market shifts and income decline over the past four decades."

Specifically, policymakers should consider initiatives such as "employment and training opportunities for those without a college degree, particularly in places most affected by blue-collar manufacturing and natural resource job loss."

"Ultimately, this is not a uniformly national crisis, and we are unlikely to 'Narcan' [brand name of overdose reversal drug] our way out," she argues. "Failure to consider the underlying economic causes could lead to ineffective policy strategies."

References

[1] Centers for Disease Control and Prevention (CDC), National Center for Health Statistics, "Compressed Mortality File 1999-2015," CDC WONDER Online Database, accessed at http://wonder.cdc.gov/cmf-icd10.html, on Dec. 13, 2017; and Holly Hedegaard, Margaret Warner, and Arialdi Miniño, "Drug Overdose Deaths in the United States, 1999–2015," NCHS Data Brief, no 273 (Hyattsville, Md.: National Center for Health Statistics, 2017).

[2] F.B. Ahmad and B. Bastian, "Quarterly Provisional Estimates for Selected Indicators of Mortality, 2016–Quarter 2, 2017," CDC, National Center for Health Statistics, National

Vital Statistics System, Vital Statistics Rapid Release Program, 2017, accessed at www.cdc.gov/nchs/products/vsrr/mortality-dashboard.htm#, on Jan. 2, 2018; Note: Choose overdose death rates from the drop-down menu in the first column.

[3] Jessica Y. Ho, "The Contribution of Drug Overdose to Educational Gradients in Life Expectancy in the United States, 1992-2011," *Demography* 54, no. 3 (2017): 1175-1202.

[4] Monica Alexander, Magali Barbieri, and Mathew Kiang, "Opioid Deaths by Race in the United States, 2000-2015," paper presented at the annual meetings of the Population Association of America, Chicago, April 27-29, 2017, accessed at https://osf.io/5brg3/, on Nov. 29, 2017, DOI: 10.17605/OSF.IO/75KR2.

[5] Shannon Monnat and David L. Brown, "More Than a Rural Revolt: Landscapes of Despair and the 2016 Presidential Election," *Journal of Rural Studies* 55, no. 1 (2017): 227-37; Shannon Monnat, "Drugs, Alcohol, and Suicide Represent Growing Share of U.S. Mortality," *Carsey Research*, University of New Hampshire, Carsey School of Public Policy, National Issue Brief No. 112 (Winter 2017); and Shannon Monnat, "Deaths of Despair from the Cities to the Hollers: Explaining Spatial Differences in U.S. Drug, Alcohol, and Suicide Mortality Rates," paper presented at the annual meetings of the Population Association of America, Chicago, April 27-29, 2017.

10

Pill Mills Are Putting Patients at Risk and Letting Them Fall Through the Cracks

Malia Cole

Malia Cole is the author of the blog Laborpain, which recounts her story and struggle as a mother living with chronic pain.

In pill mills, those who suffer from chronic pain and need painkillers are often scrutinized by their pain doctors or dismissed because they are not bringing enough money to the clinic. This viewpoint discusses the case of the author's friend who lives with chronic pain because of a neck injury but was dismissed from her pain clinic because her case wasn't financially viable. Additionally, pain clinics are so focused on making money as opposed to treating patients that they tend to automatically recommend risky treatments that involve high doses of medications to every patient, including those who don't need it.

I had a doctor friend tell me that when she was in medical school the loser students chose the field of pain. It was seen as a money-making arena, rarely successful for its patients. Ambitious doctors chose other fields, where they could actually be effective.

A friend was just dumped from her pain clinic for remaining steady on her treatment plan for many years. She has a neck injury, two children and runs her own full-time practice. She found a med that works for her, and has been taking it at a low dose without incident.

"My Story: Pain Clinics are Money Mills," by Malia Cole, National Pain Report, www.nationalpainreport.com, August 14, 2013. Reprinted by permission.

Dream patient, right? Evidently, no. She doesn't need expensive, experimental procedures. She isn't making her pain clinic any real money and they need to make space for patients who need their services (i.e. desperate and have some insurance cash to spend). She is now struggling to find a clinic that will take her. Her life will be turned inside-out if she cannot get the medication she needs.

Pain clinics are failing our community. I'm sure you have heard at least one story about the pill mills, and they certainly exist. But the demonizing story you are likely to hear is too simple and has made things impossible for those of us trying to get real treatment. Many general practitioners no longer prescribe pain medications, they don't like the liability. So if you have a chronic pain disease, you are sent into the pain clinic system.

Let's use my experience as an example: I have a condition called Sphincter of Oddi (SOD3). One of my digestive valves is misfiring—closing when it shouldn't—causing my entire system to back up. It hurts like hell, all day, every day.

I see the top GI specialist in the country and he does not have a cure for me right now. My pain, and its cause, is very different from that of fibromyalgia, RA or a back injury—it is called binary pain. It is rare, but not unheard of. I have been with my pain clinic for almost 2 years now and I still have to explain what SOD is at *every* appointment.

Without knowing anything about my disease, my pain clinic had a list of recommended treatments for me at my very first appointment: take gabapentin, do physical therapy twice a week in their clinic, and undergo steroid block injections.

I have discovered that this is what they recommend to everyone who comes to them, no matter their diagnosis. I don't pretend to know why, but I suspect those injections make them a pretty penny. I did each of these things, the injections three times. When the third round made my pain worse, the doctor commented that he *hadn't thought that treatment would work for me!*

Along with the expensive treatments, I get a lecture *each* visit about the horrors of using opioid pain medications. They simply must get me off of the one medication that actually works; the one thing that has kept me out of my bed and enjoying my girls for the last 7 years.

I have told them again and again, that unless they can find something that actually works, I will continue with the medication. However, if the war on drugs is successful at limiting the use if these medications for patients in good standing, it won't be an option for me much longer.

I rarely see my actual doctor (he is one of the top 25 pain docs in the country), the clinic uses nurse practitioners and assistants to run the day-to-day appointments. I have yet to have an appointment where the nurse has actually read my chart before meeting with me. Every time I have a procedure with my doctor, I have to tell him who I am, and describe my condition and past treatments, while lying face down on the surgical table. They must see thousands of patients a year within their 8 clinic system.

It is a money-making mill, and it is my only hope. Most pain clinics are much like this. If you switch, or *doctor shop*, too often they decide you are a *med seeker* and you can no longer get in anywhere. They have us by the balls and they know it, no customer service required.

This is all to say that something has got to change.

Contrary to the guilty-until-proven-guilty way we are treated by our pain doctors, we did not choose to have chronic pain disease and we deserve the same kind, thoughtful treatment given to those with other conditions, like diabetes or heart disease.

Every patient should get an individualized treatment plan based on their actual diagnosis. Doctors should spent time with their patients, actually getting to know them and their potential for drug abuse. The end game should be bringing comfort to people who desperately need it, not filling pockets with cash.

It is time to submit editorials, write to our representatives and advocate for ourselves, or continue to accept things as they are, in quiet desperation.

11

What Does Declaring the Opioid Crisis a Public Health Emergency Entail?

Greg Allen and Amita Kelly

Greg Allen is a Miami correspondent for NPR, and Amita Kelly serves as senior digital editor at NPR's national desk.

President Trump has declared the opioid epidemic a public health emergency and vowed to do everything in his power to fix it. As part of the plan, the Trump administration launched a campaign to bring awareness to the crisis, it made it easier for people in remote locations to find help, and it streamlined the hiring process of health care professionals who deal with addiction. Nevertheless, many argue that his plan falls short of the actions needed to help people suffering from opioid addiction. Critics lament that not enough money is being allocated to the fight against the opioid crisis.

President Trump declared a public health emergency to deal with the opioid epidemic Thursday, freeing up some resources for treatment. More than 140 Americans die every day from an opioid overdose, according to the Centers for Disease Control and Prevention.

"We are currently dealing with the worst drug crisis in American history," Trump said, adding, "it's just been so long in the making. Addressing it will require all of our effort."

"We can be the generation that ends the opioid epidemic," he said.

Trump also directed agency and department heads to use all appropriate emergency authorities to reduce the number of deaths caused by the opioid crisis.

Trump spoke personally about his brother Fred who struggled with alcoholism and died in his 40s. Because of him, Trump said, he had never tried alcohol or cigarettes. "He would tell me 'don't drink, don't drink,' " Trump said. "He had a very, very, very tough life because of alcohol."

The administration will also launch an ad campaign so that young people can see "the devastation and ruination [drugs cause] people and people's lives."

The move stops short of declaring the crisis a national emergency, which Trump first said in August that he would declare. He repeated that pledge this week. But the White House said it determined that declaring a public health emergency was more appropriate than a national emergency.

Dr. Andrew Kolodny, co-director of the Opioid Policy Research Collaboration at Brandeis University's Heller School, calls the announcement "very disappointing." Without funding for new addiction treatment, he says, declaring a public health emergency isn't enough. "This is not a plan," he says. "The administration still has no plan" for dealing with opioids, he says.

After taking office, Trump created a commission to study the opioid crisis, headed by New Jersey Gov. Chris Christie. In an interim report, the commission called on the president to declare a national emergency under either the Public Health Service Act or the Stafford Act. Doing so, the commission said, could free up funds for treatment, ensure wider access to the anti-overdose drug naloxone and improve monitoring of opioid prescriptions to prevent abuse.

Public health emergencies expire after 90 days, although the administration says they can easily be renewed. The designation gives the administration access to the Public Health Emergency Fund, but that fund is nearly empty.

In outlining its opioid plan, administration officials highlighted four areas. It allows expanded access to telemedicine services, giving doctors the ability to prescribe medications to treat addiction to those in remote locations. It speeds the hiring process for medical professionals working on opioids. And it allows funds in programs for dislocated workers and people with HIV/AIDS to be used to treat their addictions.

Dr. Keith Humphreys, a professor of psychiatry at Stanford University and a former adviser in the Obama administration, calls the Trump administration's response "pathetic," saying it mostly repurposes long-existing public health programs. Humphreys notes that aside from the emergency declaration, there is little that was recommended by the White House commission in the president's plan.

The commission had also recommended rapidly increasing treatment capacity for recovering addicts by granting Medicaid waivers, mandating educational initiatives at medical and dental schools to tighten opioid prescribing, and funding a program to expand access to medications used to treat addictions.

In a briefing Thursday, the administration said some of these initiatives are underway. The Food and Drug Administration has already expanded education requirements around prescribing opioids, officials said. Just this week, the FDA director told a congressional committee that the agency will begin working to promote medication-assisted treatment—using methadone, buprenorphine or naltrexone to help addicts in recovery— although that initiative doesn't carry any additional funding.

The final report of the White House's commission on opioids is due next week. On Thursday, Christie praised the president for what he called "bold action."

Christie said, "The President is showing an unprecedented commitment to fighting this epidemic and placing the weight of the Presidency behind saving lives across the country."

The biggest question mark surrounding the president's plan for addressing opioids involves money. Congress is currently spending $500 million a year on addiction treatment programs, but that money runs out next year. The administration says it will work with Congress in the budgeting process to find new money to fund addiction treatment programs. This week, a group of Democratic senators introduced a bill that would provide more than $45 billion for opioid abuse prevention, surveillance and treatment. Not coincidentally, that is the same amount of money Republican sponsors included for preventing opioid abuse in bills that would have repealed the Affordable Care Act.

Humphreys, a former official in the Office of National Drug Control Policy, says that if the president is serious about opioids, he should endorse that bill. Another option would be to restore a funding cut proposed for Substance Abuse and Mental Health Services Administration, the agency within the Department of Health and Human Services that oversees addiction treatment programs. In its 2018 budget, the Trump administration is proposing cutting the agency's budget by nearly $400 million.

12

Efforts to Make Naloxone Widely Available Are More Difficult than Anticipated

Jake Harper

Jake Harper is a reporter and programmer at WFYI/Side Effects Public Media in Indianapolis.

Different measures are being introduced to fight the opioid crisis, and among them is a call from the US surgeon general Jerome Adams for everyone to learn how to use naloxone and to carry it with them in case they encounter an opioid overdose. Naloxone is a countermeasure to an opioid overdose and as such it can save many lives. Yet this strategy is problematized by the fact that it is not accessible. Acquiring it requires a prescription, which is expensive, and past efforts to make it available to people who do not suffer from drug addiction disorders have failed.

It was a scheduling mishap that led Kourtnaye Sturgeon to help save someone's life. About four months ago, Sturgeon drove to downtown Indianapolis for a meeting. She was a week early.

"I wasn't supposed to be there," she said.

Heading back to the office, she saw people gathered around a car that had veered to the side of the road. Sturgeon pulled over to see if she could help. A man told her there was nothing she could do, Sturgeon said. Two men had overdosed on opioids and appeared to be dead.

"The Surgeon General Wants Us All To Carry Narcan, But It Can Be Hard To Get," by Jake Harper, Side Effects, April 20, 2018. Reprinted by permission.

"I kind of recall saying, 'No man, I've got Narcan,'" she said, referring to the brand-name version of the overdose antidote naloxone. "Which sounds so silly, but I'm pretty sure that's what came out."

Sturgeon had the drug with her because she works for Overdose Lifeline, a non-profit devoted to distributing naloxone. She sprayed a dose of the drug up the driver's nose, and waited for it to take effect. About a minute later, she said, the paramedics showed up.

"As they were walking towards us, the driver started slowly moving," she said. Both people survived.

Earlier this month, U.S. Surgeon General Jerome Adams issued an advisory. More Americans he said, should know how to use naloxone, the opioid overdose antidote, and carry it with them in case they encounter someone who has overdosed on heroin or other opioids.

The advisory includes the tagline, "Be Prepared. Get Naloxone. Save a life." The idea is that lay responders—people who may encounter an overdose before police or EMS arrive—play a critical role in saving lives.

But actually getting a hold of naloxone can be difficult. Many pharmacies and local health departments don't stock it, and not everyone can afford it.

Normally, a doctor would have to prescribe naloxone, a prescription drug, for the intended recipient, such as a person who uses heroin. Corey Davis, an attorney for the National Health Law Program, says that the stigma of addiction creates a barrier.

"A person at risk of overdose often times won't go to their doctor and say, "Hey doc, why don't you write me a naloxone prescription?'" he said.

Legalizing Access

Every state and Washington, D.C. have passed laws to increase naloxone access for friends and family members of people who use drugs or bystanders. Davis found that most states allow third-party prescriptions which let doctors prescribe naloxone to someone other than the person at risk of an overdose. Many states also allow doctors to issue standing orders to pharmacies to dispense naloxone to anyone meeting certain criteria, such as having a substance use disorder. And organizations such as non-profit groups or local health departments can also dispense naloxone in many states, a process known as lay distribution.

Some states, including Jerome Adams' home state of Indiana, have issued state-wide standing orders. Indiana allows pharmacies, local health departments or nonprofits that register with the state and follow certain requirements to dispense the drug to anyone walking in their doors.

Indiana increased access to naloxone thanks in part to advocacy from Justin Phillips. Phillips' 20-year-old son Aaron passed away in 2013 from a heroin overdose.

"I didn't know there was such a drug as naloxone," she said. "We were not prepared at all for that potential intervention for someone like Aaron."

Hoping to prevent other parents from losing a child to an overdose, she started Overdose Lifeline and pushed lawmakers to pass a law, dubbed Aaron's Law, allowing for third-party prescription and ultimately the statewide standing order. It was first enacted in 2015 and Jerome Adams signed Indiana's standing order in 2016 while serving at the state's health commissioner.

But Philips said two years later, many people are still unaware of the law, including pharmacists, which is important: Pharmacies must register with the Indiana State Department of Health to dispense naloxone under the statewide standing order.

Only about half of them do. According to the Indiana Professional Licensing Agency, there are 1,364 active pharmacies in Indiana. Information posted by ISDH shows that 628 of those are registered to dispense naloxone. A spokesperson for ISDH wrote in an email that 115 Wal-Mart pharmacies were missing from that total because they hadn't yet completed their 2017 reports.

And even in places where pharmacies are allowed to distribute the drug to lay people, they may not always do so. A recent investigation by the New York Times found that half of New York City pharmacies listed with the city as places that dispense naloxone without a prescription, did not have the drug in stock, and some required people to have a prescription to get it.

Cost Barriers

And then there's the cost. Naloxone prices have increased in recent years and Phillips said in Indiana, two doses of naloxone run between $75 and $150. Side Effects went to two drug stores in Indianapolis, which charged between $80 and $135.

"It's expensive," said Brad Ray, a researcher at Indiana University's School of Public and Environmental Affairs. "People who are users are scraping money together to buy drugs, they're not prepared to buy naloxone with that money."

Several U.S. Senators have signed on to a letter urging Health and Human Services Secretary Alex Azar to negotiate with drug companies to lower the price of naloxone, but according to The Hill, so far it seems Azar has not started that process.

A spokesperson for HHS said that the department had not yet received the letter. "We are working to ensure that there is adequate competition for naloxone, which would lead to lower pricing," they wrote in an email. HHS did not provide further details.

Outreach

For people who can't afford the drug, Ray said government and nonprofits can help. Indiana's health department used federal and state funds to purchase nearly 14,000 naloxone kits since 2016, the state reported. The state distributes those free doses through county health departments. But nearly half of Indiana counties didn't request kits. Those that did distributed the vast majority of the kits to first responders.

Research from Indiana University's Fairbanks School of Public Health also found that many doses intended for lay responders were actually handed out to first responders, perhaps because of shortages among emergency services agencies.

The county health departments that participate, Justin Phillips said, need to work hard to get naloxone to people who might use it. People who use drugs, after all, may not feel comfortable going to the government for naloxone.

"You really need to have relationships with the families that are affected, with the individuals who are suffering from opioid use disorder," said Phillips. "Those are difficult relationships to build."

Both Phillips and Ray said that syringe exchange programs are an important way to engage people who use drugs and distribute naloxone to people who need it. Scott County, a small rural county in southern Indiana, has operated a syringe exchange program since 2015. As of March 2018, Scott County had distributed 1512 naloxone kits, second only to Marion County, the state's most populous county.

But although the state legalized such programs in 2015, counties have struggled to launch and maintain them. There are currently eight syringe exchange programs operating in the state.

"Getting it in the hands of users — that's the trick we need to figure out," Ray said.

Corey Davis said there is one change that could really help. The Food and Drug Administration should make naloxone an over-the-counter medication to make it easier to access and distribute. FDA Commissioner Scott Gottlieb has the authority to do so, Davis said, but so far he has chosen not to exercise that authority, nor has a manufacturer brought an over-the-counter version of the medication to market.

"It's frustrating," he said.

13

Can Grassroots Movements Solve the Opioid Crisis?

Sarah Freeman-Woolpert

Sarah Freeman-Woolpert is the assistant editor for the Journal of Resistance Studies. *She is based in Washington, DC.*

With the latest wave of addiction-related activism, "recovery activists" have shifted their focus from raising awareness about addiction to pushing for urgent and concrete action to prevent more lives from being lost. Today's activists are more involved in politics than ever, and they're making an effort to include people of various backgrounds and races in the movement. Through creating a more inclusive and confrontational movement that works to destigmatize addiction and pursue tangible policy gains, the grassroots activists working today could play an important role in bringing an end to the opioid crisis.

Almost a decade after beginning his recovery from heroin addiction, Brett Bramble is undertaking a new challenge. Accompanied by his dog Domino and a small group of fellow activists, Bramble set off on foot in mid-January on a six-month-long, 2,400-mile journey from Florida to Maine. His walk seeks to raise visibility, foster conversations and find solutions to the skyrocketing rates of opioid addiction and overdose that have

"Amid opioid epidemic, 'recovery activists' shape a powerful grassroots movement," by Sarah Freeman-Woolpert, Waging Nonviolence, February 26, 2018, https://wagingnonviolence.org/feature/opioid-epidemic-recovery-activist-movement/. Licensed under CC BY 4.0 International.

become a nationwide public health emergency in recent years, killing over 140 Americans a day.

"For me, it all started when my sister died from a heroin overdose [nearly four years ago]," Bramble said. "She only started using in the last three months of her life. That's all it took."

Bramble's walk is one piece within a broader "recovery activist" movement that has been gaining momentum around the nation over the past decade. Led by people living in recovery or still facing addiction—along with family members whose loved ones died from overdose—the movement is becoming increasingly organized by targeting a variety of actors, drawing in key stakeholders and incorporating a range of tactics to pressure for change. Activists are becoming more strategic in their actions—staging rallies and die-ins across the country, drafting petitions and launching lawsuits.

One such activist is Nan Goldin, a 64-year-old photographer in recovery from addiction to OxyContin. In January, Goldin and her group, Prescription Addiction Intervention Now, or PAIN, launched a petition targeting Purdue Pharma and its owners, the multi-billion dollar Sackler family. With nearly 25,000 signatures gathered so far, they are demanding that Purdue fund recovery services, opioid addiction education and public dispensers of Narcan, the emergency medicine dispensed to counter a drug overdose.

Goldin's petition and Bramble's walk are evidence that the recovery movement is shifting from raising awareness of addiction to pressuring for immediate, tangible action that saves lives. According to Dean LeMire, a New Hampshire-based activist in recovery, "The movement exists in waves." The first wave involves standing up, identifying oneself as someone living in recovery, and thereby showing people that recovery is possible. The second wave, he explained, is telling elected officials: "We need dollars for this stuff." That means educating the general public about recovery services and building the political will to allocate adequate funding to prevention and recovery.

This "second wave" shift is creating an increasingly mobilized, politically-active base of recovery advocates and activists. Their work has included educating and registering voters—particularly people who are facing addiction or are in recovery—as well as pressuring for legislative change, funding for recovery services and corporate accountability. While such efforts have led to the creation of initiatives like the 2016 Comprehensive Addiction and Recovery Act, or CARA—which funds prevention, treatment and recovery initiatives nationally—much more is needed to address the scale of the growing epidemic.

At the same time, the movement's so-called "first wave" efforts —reducing prejudice and increasing awareness of addiction—is far from complete. Ryan Hampton, a prominent voice in the recovery movement, compared the stigma surrounding addiction to the social ostracism people faced during the HIV/AIDS epidemic in the 1980s. Much like back then, "the shame keeps people silent," he explained. "People are dying now from overdose because they're mortified to come out and identify as a drug user."

Hampton said his life changed when he watched the 2013 film *The Anonymous People*, a documentary featuring the stories of people living in long-term recovery from drugs and alcohol. Having confronted his own addiction to heroin, Hampton started the Voices Project in 2017, which encourages people to "come out" and share their recovery stories, using social media as a platform for people to connect with and support one another.

Despite steps towards destigmatizing addiction, the movement faces a somber uphill battle, as its leading participants must also deal with the ongoing challenges of long-term recovery. "For everybody who is in recovery, it is a daily fight to [survive]," Hampton said. Still, in many ways, that struggle is aided by channeling grief into action. That's one reason Hampton was able to register 100 new "recovery voters" in just three weeks time by simply saying: "Are you sick of your friends dying? Well here's something you can do."

Tactics and Visibility

So far, some of the movement's major actions have promoted visibility and solidarity among people in recovery, often through coalitions with other campaigns. Since 2014, Families of Addicts has brought together thousands of people for the annual "Rally 4 Recovery" in Dayton, Ohio, which includes a 5k run, a raffle and a balloon launch, as well as resource tables for people facing addiction.

On the national level, activists came together in October 2015 with a coalition of over 450 organizations from around the country for the UNITE to Face Addiction rally and concert on the National Mall in Washington, D.C. The rally was hosted by Facing Addiction, a national organization that advocates for the over 85 million Americans affected by addiction around the country.

Some of these actions, which aim to destigmatize addiction, have taken place on social media, where Hampton plays a central role in mobilizing numbers to respond quickly when a situation arises. For example, when Arizona House Majority Leader Kelly Townsend posted offensive comments about drug users on Facebook in 2016, Hampton quickly shared her contact information on his page, which had around 40,000 followers at the time. According to Hampton, she was flooded with 1,500 phone calls in just three hours. But rather than shame her or call her names, Hampton recalled people saying things like, "'Hey, I just want you to know I'm in recovery, here's who I am today.' Or, 'My kid died of an overdose. He was a good kid. Let me tell you about him.'"

These actions played an important role in humanizing the issue and gaining a spotlight to tell the personal stories behind recovery and addiction. "We saw that storytelling—kicking down those closet doors—could have a massive impact," Hampton said.

Meanwhile, other actions have fallen more squarely under the "second wave" category of mobilizing political pressure. In 2015, activists with the Weed for Warriors project dumped pill bottles and syringes in front of the White House lawn to drawn attention to the overprescription of opioid drugs to wounded veterans. Then, last May, protesters held a "die-in" at the New Hampshire State House when U.S. Health and Human Services Secretary Tom Price visited the capitol.

As with the reaction to Townsend's insensitive remarks, many of these direct actions occur through mobilization over social media. When one woman shopping at the cosmetic store Sephora discovered a line of makeup products called "Druggie," she posted about it on social media, creating an instant internet sensation. The incident quickly went viral, and activists again flooded the company with phone calls and social media posts condemning the product line. Sephora eventually discontinued the product, and—according to Hampton—he and other organizers within the movement were contacted by a public relations firm asking them to "please call off the dogs."

While these incidents make headlines and gain public attention, much of the movement-building work is comparatively slow and incremental, enacted more at the local and state levels. This includes seeking government support and funding for harm reduction strategies, including the formation of recovery community organizations, or RCOs, which are nonprofit organizations that plan recovery advocacy efforts, as well as community education and outreach. Activists are also pushing for syringe exchange programs, increased health care access for drug users, and safe injection sites like the ones San Francisco plans to open in July —the first in the nation.

Much of this may not look like activism, LeMire acknowledged —at least not in the sense of crowds swarming in the streets, chanting and demanding change from the government. "This is all slow-cooker stuff," he said. "But none of [these] formal supports were around three years ago, so I know we're headed in the right direction."

Mobilizing a Wide Spectrum of Allies

A significant advantage to the recovery activist movement is the sheer number of people it stands to reach. One in three people in America are directly affected by addiction, either through personal experience as a user or through a close friend or family member. The movement therefore holds immense potential to mobilize a wide range of stakeholders, a base of supporters, which—unlike many current movements—spans both sides of the political divide. According to a Pew exit poll conducted after the 2016 election, both Republicans and Democrats consider addiction to be a "very big problem."

"I've met parents who were enthusiastic Trump supporters because they had been fed the message of building the wall and keeping the drugs from Mexico," Hampton said, adding that he would then tell parents to think about how a "repeal and replace" of health care legislation would affect their son or daughter. "It's like a lightbulb goes off in their heads, and they don't want to see another four years of Donald Trump."

President Trump has repeatedly declared the opioid epidemic a major problem, but does not allocate funding for it to be systematically addressed. In October 2017, the Trump administration declared the opioid epidemic a public health emergency, but did not request emergency funding from Congress and did not declare a national state of emergency, which would have allowed states to use the federal Disaster Relief Fund to address the crisis.

Recovery activists described how the escalating crisis of addiction and overdose—as well as the government's inaction to address it—is increasing the movement's sense of urgency to take more extreme measures. People have long sought to earn a seat at the table with important decision makers, both Hampton and LeMire explained, but now they may be compelled to take more direct or confrontational measures.

"We're just getting a pat on the head," Hampton said. "It's an affirmative action play that policymakers need to have that seat for us, but don't actually have to listen to us. We're sick of that. We don't need a seat at that table if that's how we're going to be treated. People are building their own tables, and that's more powerful."

LeMire echoed Hampton's sentiments, saying, "We finally got a seat at the table, but this president is hostile to any social or mental health services. People are trying to give him more chances, thinking that maybe he will listen. But now we are seeing activists starting to understand that we need to just totally refuse this administration. We need to take to the streets."

The shift towards direct action is a challenging one to make for a community so frequently criminalized. People have identified as "advocates" in recent years and sought to make change through official channels, but many are skeptical of making the shift towards more confrontational "activist" tactics. Hampton said that when he started using the word "activist," people groaned and asked him, "Are we there yet?" He told them, "I don't think we have a choice."

"For so long we have been trying to ingratiate ourselves to a society that distrusted us, to decision makers who distrusted us," LeMire said, adding that people have long been trying to counter the perception that they might "steal your wallet." But now, he reflected, "We have to break away from this."

While the stigma against people facing addiction serves as a major challenge to the development of an activist movement, one important set of allies is trying to change that: parents who have lost their children to overdose. The testimonies of these parents appeals to public sympathy and outrage, making the movement more relatable to the average person and increasing public pressure for political change.

"Most of the [parents of loss] that I've met have dedicated their lives to ending overdoses," Hampton said. "They've made treatment more accessible, taken on Big Pharma and taken on big policy leaders on Capitol Hill."

These parents and family members are playing a vital and visible role in the movement, countering some of the negative associations that can be tied to recovery activism with the power of their personal stories, which help to humanize the abstract, demonized image of an addict.

A Generational Shift

Another major challenge the movement faces exists within the divided approaches to recovery. Hampton described this as both a generational and cultural change within the recovery community, from abstinence-only programs to those focused on "harm reduction."

"In my personal experience, some of the hardest challengers of the movement have been from within the recovery community itself, mostly the 12-step group," Hampton said. While these programs have helped a lot of people on their journey to recovery, including Hampton, they represent a different approach to overcoming addiction that is shifting with the new wave of activism and advocacy today.

Twelve-step programs promote full abstinence from drug use, and often highlight the role of religion and the importance of anonymity. The emerging recovery movement, on the other hand, encourages people to "come out" and share their recovery stories. It promotes an approach to recovery that seeks to "meet people where they're at," LeMire said, "which may well be face-down in a public restroom or hotel."

This new approach advocates syringe exchange and other services that allow people to continue using drugs, but in a safer, more controlled environment. According to LeMire, this creates a rift between the two approaches because both look at each other and think, "You're killing people."

Meanwhile, their concern is real because people are dying. Movement organizers are highly vulnerable themselves to overdose. Numerous advocates and activists have already died, and many other potential supporters are incarcerated or living on the margins of society. "In the past 19 months I've had 13 friends die," Hampton said in December. "It's not a question of when it's gonna happen anymore, it's a question of who."

Two months later, Hampton had lost four more friends.

Challenging the Movement as a "Sea of White"

An important consideration for the movement to achieve long-term, systemic change is its ability to be representative of all people facing addiction. This means, according to activists at the forefront, that the movement must also recognize its own implicit biases, particularly the predominance of white, middle- and upper-class people it engages.

Although the movement is gaining ground today for criticizing the pharmaceutical industry and government policies around addiction, the criminalization of drug users began long before Nixon's "War on Drugs," with the persecution of black and Latino communities, and the targeting of jazz musicians like Louis Armstrong and Billie Holiday by Commissioner Harry J. Anslinger, who headed the Federal Bureau of Narcotics from 1930-1962. This history is one reason why LeMire is pushing the current recovery movement to recognize and incorporate the dangers faced specifically by communities of color.

"The rallies and protests—they're a sea of white," LeMire said. "[People of color] are almost totally missing from the movement, but they have the most to lose." This shapes one of the movement's ongoing challenges, addressing the addiction crisis while elevating the voices of marginalized communities.

This poses a conundrum to the movement's current successes, and requires the white, educated people within the movement to question the reasons many people have been sympathetic to their stories. LeMire, who once served as the face of an awareness campaign for Narcan, the emergency medication used to reverse an opioid overdose, said it was telling that they chose someone like him—"a white, bespectacled college grad."

"Minority communities," he explained, "have historically been disproportionately mistreated—not just untreated, but mistreated —as a result of the drug policies that created this situation." A greater understanding of the way race and privilege have affected the criminalization of drug use and the services available to drug users could lead to what LeMire called the movement's "third wave."

If the second wave of the movement establishes more understanding, compassion and education surrounding recovery, it will only be accomplished, according to LeMire, "by addressing deep-rooted injustices," particularly those that have been brought to the forefront under the Trump administration. Addressing the historical factors underlying the oppression of people with addiction, he concluded, "will mean passing the megaphone to those who have not yet had it."

For some, the recovery activist movement aims to help people "find ways to not die today," as LeMire put it. Yet, on a broader, systemic level, the recovery activist movement holds the potential to activate a massive, invigorated voter base on both sides of the political divide. It gives voice to those who feel powerless or unheard, and shapes the movement as one in which the fight against addiction and injustice will be led by those who have experienced it firsthand.

14

America's Punishment-Based Moral System Is a Cause of the Opioid Crisis

Abigail Ronck Hartstone

Abigail Ronck Hartstone is an editorial consultant for the Tow Center for Digital Journalism and Harvard Kennedy School's Shorenstein Center. She previously was a contributor to the Atavist and How We Get To Next.

America's "war on drugs"—a campaign to reduce the illegal drug trade and stop drug use, which began with the Nixon administration in 1971—has created a society that treats drug use as a moral issue and stigmatizes drug users. This punitive approach to drug control has done nothing to prevent the opioid crisis and has in fact prevented drug users from accessing resources that might help them. However, policymakers may finally be coming around to harm reduction strategies, such as offering easy access to naloxone and clean needles.

Four years ago, I stood outside a Burger King in Washington Heights with a 17-year-old kid named Eric Dorris. We were giving out overdose first-aid kits with naloxone, a drug that when sprayed up the nose of someone who has overdosed gives them the breath of life by knocking opioids from the body's receptors. The public bathroom inside the fast food restaurant on the corner of New York City's 181st Street and St. Nicholas Avenue—the

"Street Wisdom Might Win the War on Drugs," by Abigail Ronck Hartstone, How We Get To Next, June 21, 2016, https://howwegettonext.com/street-wisdom-might-win-the-war-on-drugs-6635214d82a0. Licensed under CC BY-SA 4.0.

intersection of old-fashioned heroin addiction and the latest trend in opioid abuse, prescription pain pills—was a well-known shooting gallery. The corner's adjoining sidewalks were the best place in the Heights to buy anything from OxyContin to Vicodin. Back then, it was somewhere people would listen to our overdose evangelism. Some people we spoke to that day already knew about naloxone. They even carried their kit with a little note taped to it that read: "If you find me blue, spray this in my nose."

Dorris was a lanky kid dressed in skinny jeans and a hoodie. While friends from his alternative high school in the West Village had elected to study things like glassblowing or origami, he had an interest in neurosurgery and was interning with the New York Harm Reduction Coalition. I was a fledgling journalist who had just learned about naloxone; Dorris was already planning to carry it to parties where his peers would crush up, snort, or otherwise ingest pills from their parents' medicine cabinets to get high. He knew that opioid overdose is one liability that is near 100 percent preventable.

The little nasal device that could save lives on the spot was a telling symbol—its near anonymity at the time a potent reminder of America's total lack of interest in helping drug users save their own lives. Developed in 1961 and approved by the FDA in 1971 to treat overdose, naloxone was virtually unknown to just about everyone in 2012, even doctors. It wasn't stocked at pharmacies and was still a controlled substance in most states. It had a very sparse Wikipedia page, and no one cared much for offering it to back-alley junkies on a widespread basis. Drug users at risk of overdose, and their friends and families that worried about them, couldn't really get it in the United States.

But as America's overdose fatalities exceeded 47,000 annually in 2014, with opioids involved in some 29,000 of those deaths, wealthier suburban addicts transitioning from pain pills to cheaper heroin have by now reframed the country's image of overdose. By all accounts, the traditional "war on drugs" has failed—the opioid overdose death rate more than quadrupling since the year 2000.

It's our kids, the friends of Eric Dorris, that have given addiction a new, sympathetic face.

Just as the epidemic is a key campaign issue in the 2016 presidential election, last week the American Medical Association clarified new opioid policies at its annual meeting in Chicago that encourage doctors to co-prescribe opioid painkillers with overdose reversal drugs like naloxone, proposing that insurers cover the "overdose antidote" with little or no cost-sharing.

The tide has turned. Finally—finally—it seems the United States is ready to look toward a decades-old harm reduction movement that makes it safer to use drugs and first and foremost champions saving lives. Historically, that concept has been unpalatable to Americans, maybe even considered morally wrong. But as U.S. drug policy has failed to curb a climb toward one of the highest drug-related mortality rates worldwide at 4.6 times the global average, a softer way is in order. That means more access to naloxone, more clean-needle clinics to stop the spread of HIV and hepatitis C—essentially, safe spaces to use drugs—and a big win for grassroots advocates who came long before Eric Dorris and his generation, and have been laying this foundation for decades.

Colloquial narrative among drug-user advocates pins the roots of harm reduction in the United States to Chicago in 1990. Just after 7 p.m. on a Tuesday, 13 heroin addicts sat around a table over sweet rolls and coffee. Visually, they were a diverse group: men of different races and ethnicities. A handful of them were HIV positive. Each had been involved in 12-step recovery groups but, for one reason or another, found himself at this diner after feeling unwelcome or stigmatized. The goal was to deal with the meaning of the name they had chosen for themselves: The Chicago Recovery Alliance, one of the earliest harm reduction groups in the country.

It could have taken hours. That was until John Szyler, a heroin addict of 35 years who went on to overdose and die in 1996, opened with this: "Any positive change. That's recovery."

There was silence, until someone else echoed, "Sh*t, yeah, that's it."

Dan Bigg, who was 28 at the time, said: "And suddenly we were all in the same boat together."

With a masters in psychology and one nasty case of distaste for the industrial addiction complex, Bigg was a self-described "happy drug user" back then. But by 1996, energized by Szyler's death, he got serious. Losing his friend to a heroin overdose was enough reason to start thinking about what he could do to start saving lives. After researching pilot naloxone programs abroad in developing countries like Vietnam, India, and Thailand, with the help of a few doctor friends he was the first to bring it to the Chicago streets illegally. The Chicago Recovery Alliance debuted its community-based naloxone program in the spring of 1997.

"Are people willing to step back and say, 'Our moralism is killing us?" Bigg asked me. "Do you make a reckoning that you are condemning groups of people to death based on behavior?"

Bigg faced opposition from the very beginning. "For the life of me I could not figure out why," he said. "If you wanted to create something to test the fabric of society, to see if we would go forth and save someone's life from accidental death [if we could], naloxone would be it."

Even some of his harm reduction peers felt medical treatment for drug users should be left to emergency-room doctors and paramedics, who have been carrying naloxone for decades. Bigg distributed it anyway, driving around the city in a nondescript van of unpainted aluminum with a small blue and red arrow logo on its side. He even made house calls, reversing a number of lethal overdoses himself. After finding someone in a heavy nod, unresponsive to stimulation and blue in the lips from lack of oxygen, naloxone usually wakes a person who is overdosing in three to five minutes. "The person just starts to breathe like a baby," he said. If administered within a 30- to 90-minute window, it's enough to prevent death even if no additional care is provided. It has no side effects other than bringing someone with opioids in their system into immediate withdrawal.

By the year 2000, overdose deaths in Cook County, Illinois, had dropped 30 percent, said Bigg. This seemed to stall a 12-year increase in rising overdose rates in Chicago.

In 2001, as the United States saw a resurgence of heroin-based overdoses, a pilot program in San Francisco put some science behind what Bigg had started. After recruiting a small number of street addicts to monitor the safety of training injection drug-using partners to perform CPR and administer naloxone in the event of an overdose, researchers gathered data around 20 heroin overdoses during six months of follow-up. Study participants performed CPR 16 of those times, administered naloxone in 15 cases, and did one or the other in 19. All overdose victims survived. The point was: Addicts were willing and capable of helping each other.

Despite positive results, the movement had its critics—most notably the formidable drug czar under George W. Bush, Bertha Madras. After reviewing the research, she deemed it insufficient for enacting public policy and remained an adamant resistor of take-home naloxone programs. In a phone interview with me in 2012, she said harm reductionists had long ago nicknamed her "Dr. Death." Even years later, she stood by her initial reaction. "For me, it really is callous to rescue a person from a near death experience and just leave them without professional intervention that can help them to recover and try to address the underlying issues that go with addiction," she said.

By 1996, an army of harm reduction field workers and clinicians had initiated a host of community-based programs that offered naloxone to drug users, their families, and friends, reporting the distribution of over 50,000 kits (often illegally, as in many states it was still considered a controlled substance) and more than 10,000 death reversals by 2008.

This work, sometimes covert, paved the way for people like Dr. Alexander Walley, who after a chain of heroin overdoses in Quincy, Massachusetts, in 2010 helped expand the state's naloxone program to equip the entire Quincy police force. It also inspired

Bill Matthews, a former classical musician who once worked for the United Nations but by 2011 was spending his days trying to convince principals to let him into schools to speak about overdose prevention. (Now, in the Dansville Central School District in western New York, school nurses keep naloxone among the headache medicine they dispense.) It challenged the climate of abstinent-only recovery for those like health care professional Wanda Zanetti, who worked at a drug treatment center in New York State. There she promoted training around naloxone, saying that 80 percent of her patients opt-in to receive the kit—imagining they might one day use it on themselves or a friend.

It was all this that forced a 2012 FDA conference—over 40 years after the body had approved naloxone use—in which the federal government was finally ready to listen to a little street wisdom about overdose treatment. While there was good reason to look at taking naloxone over the counter as one avenue for containing a growing national overdose epidemic, getting it into drug users' hands without a prescription would be tricky. At this time, it was only legally available with a prescription from special overdose prevention groups in 15 states and the District of Columbia under state Good Samaritan Laws that protected those who used it from criminal prosecution or civil liability when calling 911 after witnessing an overdose. Plus, naloxone had other complexities—it needs to be administered by someone else, so even if you had a prescription, the medication was likely not for you.

Madras still had oppositions; and FDA representative Andrea Leonard-Segal cautioned that the FDA does not control over-the-counter advertising. "You need to think about what a T.V. ad for naloxone might look like," she said.

And yet, perhaps louder than the detractors rang the voice of Susan Gregory, whose son had died of an accidental overdose at age 20. "My son died alone on a bathroom floor," she said. "On the other side of that door were a lot of people and a pharmacy. I didn't know about naloxone then. Why didn't I know about it?" she cried.

Four years later, now we do. To date, law enforcement departments in 36 states carry naloxone. CVS pharmacies now have the drug available over the counter in 23 states. As for the old guard monitoring the war on drugs in the White House, it's gone. The current drug czar, Michael Botticelli, is the first director of national drug control policy to be in recovery from substance abuse himself. He was a keynote speaker at the 2014 Harm Reduction Conference in Baltimore, where he explicitly offered his support for both the movement and naloxone.

All this amounts to recognition of a true crisis—and a compassionate bending to a once-staunch ethos that judged those suffering from drug addiction and the actions we take to help them.

But here's the thing: overdoses aren't just a U.S. problem. Naloxone is on the World Health Organization's List of Essential Medicines, or those considered necessary within any basic health system, for good reason. While the U.N. Office on Drugs and Crime World Drug Report 2015 confirms that North America contributes an estimated 23 percent to the number of drug-related deaths globally (which in 2013 was around 187,100), it also notes that this high figure is in part due to better monitoring and reporting around drug-related deaths in higher-income countries like the United States. In other countries, drug use and overdose data simply isn't collected.

No country in Asia or Africa conducts household surveys on drug use like we do in America and Western Europe—it's too expensive—and data collection around drug-related mortalities is very limited. Still, there are a raft of statistics showing that drugs are a global problem. The WHO estimates that 69,000 people die each year around the world from opioid overdose alone. The UNODC reports that in conjunction with the United States, the Russian Federation and China account for 48 percent of the total number of people who inject drugs globally. With 80 percent of the global opium production occurring in Afghanistan, injection drug use is also high in the nearby Middle East and North Africa. Meanwhile, overall rates of drug use in Oceania (Australia, New

Zealand, and a number of Pacific Island countries) are well above the global average, prescription opioids being much more popular than heroin in the region.

In Italy, naloxone is available in pharmacies without a prescription, and as of 2011 Scotland became the first country in the world to implement a national take-home naloxone program. A UNODC and World Health Organization 2013 discussion paper about preventing and reducing opioid overdose mortality noted that community-based naloxone distribution programs exist, to some extent or another, in over a dozen countries, including Afghanistan, Australia, Canada, China, India, Kazakhstan, Kyrgyzstan, Tajikistan, Thailand, the United Kingdom, Ukraine, and Vietnam. Many were in pilot or experimental form at the time and may have ceased operations, but others are likely to have sprung up, too.

Naloxone is currently available in hospitals in Kenya and Tanzania, but there is no access to overdose treatment for the wider population in Africa. Reminiscent of Bigg and his colleagues, though, there are boots on the ground: The national harm reduction network in Mauritius, together with the Kenyan AIDS NGOs Consortium (KANCO), used the "Support. Don't Punish" campaign as a platform for people to talk publicly about drug policy reform.

Although harm reduction is becoming more accepted across Asia where there are an estimated 3.15 million IV drug-users, punitive drug policies are still in place. China has no national program for overdose prevention, though AIDS Care China did open naloxone peer-distribution programs in Yunnan and Sichuan provinces.

In Russia, it's believed that around 90,000 people die from overdose every year. If that's true, this accounts for half of all lethal drug overdoses worldwide. Since the fall of the Soviet Union, the country—again, with opium-producer Afghanistan at its doorstep—has claimed the world's highest rate of injection drug users with 1.8 million. The Russian Federation continues to implement a zero tolerance approach to narcotics and has used anti-propaganda laws to suppress harm reduction services and advocacy.

Halting a global epidemic around fatal overdoses won't come without effort or cost. It certainly hasn't in the United States, where on average 130 people still die from them every day. The road to changing policy has been a long one, and countries that follow a similar path of resistance might meet a similar fate. There is, of course, another way.

It's a movement that found life on the streets over 25 years ago; it's an old method for treating drug users passed down by forgotten heroin addicts of yesterday. It's one that has gained an ally in a new generation of kids like Eric Dorris, who are facing the same threat of drug overdose—at worser scale. In the four years since he took up the torch and hit the streets (and high school parties) with naloxone, we've seen serious progress around overdose awareness and drug policy change in America.

To continue this trend will surely require more work, in the United States and globally. But if you're in Dan Bigg's camp—and that of advocates from so many pockets of the globe now voicing support for reducing harm for drug users—any positive change will do.

15

Pills, Heroin, and the Road to Recovery

Nicole Makris

Nicole Makris is a family nurse practitioner in Amherst, Massachusetts. She previously worked as a contributing writer for Healthline Media.

Whether an opioid is legal or illegal, heroin or a prescription pill, it operates in the same way: by blocking the brain's reception of pain signals from nerves in the body. Additionally, opioid use across the board has similar undesirable effects, including the sense of euphoria that leads to addiction and the building up of tolerance, which leads to the need for higher and higher doses. While many who can no longer access pain pills turn to heroin, those who can afford to obtain prescription opioids tend to continue doing so despite the higher cost because they are less stigmatized.

Over the past two decades, a disturbing trend has come to the attention of law enforcement officers, substance abuse counselors, and healthcare providers.

The United States has a heroin problem.

Over just six years, the number of people trying heroin for the first time nearly doubled from 90,000 in 2006 to 156,000 in 2012.

In 2000, 1,842 people died of a heroin overdose. By 2014, that number had quintupled to 10,574.

"Prescription Drugs Are Leading to Heroin Addictions," by Nicole Makris, Healthline Media, www.healthline.com, February 26, 2016. Reprinted by permission.

The White House recently noted that more Americans die from drug overdoses than from motor vehicle crashes each year.

In fact, the number of people who died from drug overdoses in 2014—approximately 47,055—was greater than the number of people who died in the peak year of the AIDS epidemic in 1995.

"Heroin use has been increasing markedly by all measures. Abuse rates are going up. Death rates are going up. The treatment rates are going up," Dr. Wilson Compton, deputy director of the National Institute on Drug Abuse (NIDA) told Healthline. "It qualifies as an epidemic by anyone's definition."

A number of theories exist to explain the rise in heroin use in recent years, including increased supply and demand, and drug trafficking.

But most public health officials and a growing number of policymakers now acknowledge that the country's rise in prescriptions for opioid-type painkillers such as Vicodin and Percocet play a major role.

"Most of the heroin users now, their first opioid exposures are the prescription drugs. That's true for at least 80 percent of today's heroin addicts," Compton said. "That's very different than 30 or 40 years ago, when the first opioid was heroin."

Opiate vs. Opioid

More than 60 percent of 2014's drug overdoses were related to opioid use.

Heroin and some legal painkillers like morphine and codeine are isolated from the opium poppy. These naturally derived painkillers are sometimes referred to as opiates.

The term opioid, once used to denote that a substance was created synthetically, is now a catch-all term for any drug that produces analgesic effects by acting on opioid receptors in the body's nervous system.

Any opioid, whether synthetic or naturally derived, functions in the same way. The body's response to pain is actually a process of stimulus and response: something sharp or hot or blunt or inflamed alerts nerves in the body to send a signal to the brain. The brain then sends back a signal to the body that the stimulus is painful.

While the neuronal pathway of opioids is somewhat complex, the drugs essentially inhibit the brain's response to painful stimuli. The stimulus makes it up to the brain, but opioids block the "ouch" response that's headed back to the body.

"The brain doesn't distinguish between heroin and prescription opioids," Compton said. "The majority of the impact of opioids are within the brain itself.

It doesn't change the pain itself, but it changes the perception of it. The pain doesn't go away. It just doesn't bother you."

Legal prescriptions for opioids are useful for acute pain like broken bones, nasty lacerations, or post-surgical pain.

But if opioids are used over time for chronic conditions, tolerance and dependence can develop.

Tolerance is the need for higher and higher doses to achieve the analgesic effect. Dependence, on the other hand, is the body's need for routine and regular doses of a substance to prevent a withdrawal syndrome.

Addiction, a more complicated psychological diagnosis, is marked not only by the physical havoc that tolerance and dependence wreak on the body, but the emotional and social toll that results from prioritizing drug use over social relationships and personal responsibilities.

Warning: Causes Euphoria

Dr. Peter Grinspoon, a family physician in Massachusetts and author of the recently released book *Free Refills,* understands addiction firsthand.

He was training as a medical student at Harvard when his girlfriend's physician father sent along a med school care package that included "a big box of Vicodin," he remembers.

"We, of course, looked up all the medications. And Vicodin said, 'Warning: causes euphoria and a false sense of well-being,'" he told Healthline. "We were destined to try it. Right? I mean, this is the worst thing to write if you don't want people to try it."

Throughout med school, his residency, and into his practice as a family doctor, Grinspoon continued to abuse prescription opioids.

"It's extremely high stress, being a doctor, combined with the unlimited access of prescription opioids for physicians," he said. "That's a very bad combination—stress and access."

In February 2005, state police and Drug Enforcement Agency officers, acting on a tip from a local pharmacist, showed up at Grinspoon's office. He lost his medical license, went to rehab, relapsed several times, and finally got clean in 2007.

Grinspoon acknowledged that his addiction caused him to make bad decisions not just for himself, but also for his patients. He admits to making deals in which he'd get a share of a patient's prescriptions as well as stealing drugs from terminally ill patients.

"The patients that I crossed the boundaries with, and that we shared prescriptions … I think I facilitated their addiction or their diversion of controlled substances," he said. "What I was prescribing, I don't know if they were taking them or selling them."

Now back in practice, Grinspoon's perspective on opioids and addiction is informed not just by his own fall from grace, but the addiction stories of others he met in recovery and rehab.

"My addiction was stopped before I progressed to heroin," he said. "A lot of people get addicted to the pills and then progress to heroin because they can't afford the pills."

He's had patients who were addicted to heroin, and has also lost patients to overdose. Grinspoon noted that the warning signs for abuse can be very non-specific.

"There were a couple really together-seeming, clean cut patients that I had no idea. I was just astounded to find out that they were using heroin every day," he said. "I feel like I have a pretty good detector for this, but I didn't detect it at all."

From Pills to Heroin

Grinspoon and Compton both acknowledge that prescribers of opioids have an important role in preventing addiction. But the pathway of addiction is not as straightforward as it might seem.

"Most of the people dying from overdose and most of the people misusing these are not those to whom the prescription is written," Compton said. "It's part of environmental availability. People are sharing the pills, or they're stolen or diverted."

The recent rise in opioid and heroin coincides with a push in the late 1990s and early 2000s by the pharmaceutical companies' introduction of new formulations of prescription opioids.

The availability of these drugs was fueled in part by a misleading marketing campaign by OxyContin maker Purdue Pharma, which promoted the extended-release form of the drug as less addictive than other opioids.

In 2007, Purdue Pharma paid $634 million in fines for its false claims. But the damage had been done. In 1991, 76 million prescriptions were written for opioids. By 2011, that number had nearly tripled to 219 million—enough to give one bottle of pills to every American over the age of 15.

A prescription for painkillers obviously doesn't evolve into heroin addiction for everyone with an ACL tear. Even those who fall into the dependence and addiction categories have limited use of heroin. Just 4 percent of people classified prescription opioid abusers progress to heroin use within five years, according to NIDA.

Still, addiction to opioid painkillers is a major risk factor for heroin use. Marijuana users are three times more likely to be addicted to heroin than people who don't use drugs. Cocaine users have a 15-fold risk.

But people addicted to prescription opioids are 40 times more likely to become addicted to heroin, according to the CDC.

"They start off with pills, and then there's a transition to heroin. Their friends and drug-using social network may help them realize that it may be available, and cheap." Compton said. "Or they find that they're unable to obtain the pills as readily."

The question of access and cost is at the crux of the transition from pills to heroin.

"In many markets, on an opioid/milligram equivalent, [heroin] is cheaper," Compton said.

Many people who abuse opioids remain wary of the stigma attached to heroin. But Grinspoon points out that addiction is a disease, and that stigma and fear might not mean much to a person whose life revolves around getting their next fix.

Grinspoon says his access to pills may have played more of a role in preventing him from trying heroin than any moral code or perception of rock bottom did.

"I could afford the pills. I was a doctor, and I was getting a lot of the pills for free," he said. "Heroin has such a stigma that I'm not sure I would have lowered myself to that as a physician. I think that might have been another line that I would never have crossed. But who knows?

With addiction you just don't know ... the addiction takes over the part of your brain that makes good decisions. After a while it certainly feels like the addiction is calling the shots. Toward the end, you become less and less in control of your behaviors."

Compton says that fear and reluctance to move to heroin is healthy, but he is wary of classifying heroin addiction as worse than opioid addiction.

"There's still many more people dying of drug overdoses related to the pills than there are related to heroin," he said.

The Road to Recovery

Across the country, acknowledgement of the heroin epidemic, and the role of prescription opioids in combatting it, has gained the attention of lawmakers.

Earlier this month, the Obama administration proposed a $1.1 billion initiative aimed at treating opioid addiction.

The National Governors Association recently decided to create guidelines aimed at reducing the type and number of prescriptions —a move that might put prescribers in a tough position but has garnered bipartisan support.

The U.S. Department of Health and Human Services targeted three key efforts last year: increased training for health professionals and prescribers; access to naloxone, an overdose-reversal drug; and expansion of Medication-Assisted Treatment (MAT), a type of recovery treatment that includes daily administration of opioid-like drugs that's proven to reduce withdrawal and relapse.

In small towns and big cities, efforts to curb the tide of opioid addiction have led to innovative solutions.

Once seen as criminal activity, hard drug use and illegal use of prescription drugs is now fostering conversations of addiction as a disease, and less harsh penalties are seen as a means of supporting recovery.

In Gloucester, Massachusetts—a community that has seen staggering increases in opioid abuse and overdose rates—police have initiated a program that allows addicts to come to the police department for help accessing recovery services.

They will not be arrested or charged with criminal activity. Instead, they'll be taken to a nearby hospital and paired with a volunteer who will help them access immediate treatment.

In the Yale-New Haven Hospital Emergency Room, a study found that opioid-dependent patients who were given access to buprenorphine (one of the opioid-like MAT drugs promoted by HHS) were significantly more likely to be in recovery treatment after 30 days than those who were simply referred to treatment.

Naloxone, an opioid overdose reversal drug, is now carried by many police officers and first responders throughout the country. In addition, CVS and Walgreens recently announced it will be available without a prescription in Ohio.

Twenty states and Washington, D.C., have now enacted so-called Good Samaritan 911 laws that grant amnesty to anyone who seeks medical help for a person who has overdosed—even if drugs are present or the caller is under the influence.

These developments are not without their criticisms.

Over 10 years, heroin use increased 114 percent in the white population and 77 percent in the middle-class income bracket. Some say that the conversation about drug use as an addiction, and the reduced penalties that come with it, are only happening because white, middle-class people are now affected.

"One the one hand it seems profoundly unfair that minorities were treated so poorly with this terrible disease," Grinspoon said. "On the other hand, the fact that the paradigm is shifting is a great thing for everybody. Because this is the way addiction should be treated: as a disease, not as something that should be punished."

Compton said that NIDA has been a longstanding proponent of combining both public health and criminal justice efforts to get people the services they need, and points out that there is a lot of overlap among addicts and prisoners—and that preventing a drug relapse is not so different from preventing recidivism.

"Public heath operating all by itself struggles with our patients dropping out of treatment. Criminal justice suffers from similar issues. Even if you bring someone into prison, they're at extraordinarily high risk when they're released if you haven't provided treatment," he said. "For those who engage in illegal risky, dangerous behavior—which is not that rare in drug abusing populations no matter what community they're from—it's by working together that we can represent the future of providing the best outcomes."

Organizations to Contact

The editors have compiled the following list of organizations concerned with the issues debated in this book. The descriptions are derived from materials provided by the organizations. All have publications or information available for interested readers. The list was compiled on the date of publication of the present volume; the information provided here may change. Be aware that many organizations take several weeks or longer to respond to inquiries, so allow as much time as possible.

Advocates for the Reform of Prescription Opioids (ARPO)
PO Box 91117
Salt Lake City, UT 84109
website: www.rxreform.org

The Advocates for the Reform of Prescription Opioids (ARPO) is an alliance between the United States and Canada founded to fight opioid drug addiction, which has plagued these two countries. The organization is made up of family members of people suffering from drug use disorder.

American Medical Association
AMA Plaza
330 N. Wabash Avenue, Suite 39300
Chicago, IL 60611-5885
phone: (312) 464-4782
website: www.end-opioid-epidemic.org

The American Medical Association is a national organization for people in the medical field. It also includes a task force (AMA Opioid Task) that was founded to help in combatting the current epidemic.

American Society of Addiction Medicine (ASAM)
11400 Rockville Pike, Suite 200
Rockville, MD 20852
phone: (301) 656-3920
email: email@ASAM.org
website: www.asam.org

The American Society of Addiction Medicine focuses on providing better care to patients with addiction. With over 5,500 health care members, ASAM wants to educate people about drug addiction and to successfully curb this disease.

Cardinal Health
7000 Cardinal Place
Dublin, OH 43017
phone: (614) 757-5000
website: www.cardinalhealth.com

Cardinal Health is a global company that provides pharmaceuticals and medical supplies to hospitals, pharmacies, the offices of physicians, and other health care entities. Its subsidiary, the Cardinal Health Opioid Action Program, offers information on how pharmaceutical companies are aiding in the fight against opioid addiction.

Generations United
25 E Street NW, 3rd Floor
Washington, DC 20001
phone: (202) 289-3979
email: gu@gu.org
website: www.gu.org

Generations United focuses on involving the elderly, youth, and children in projects like vaccination awareness and racial equity. This organization also works on helping grandparents who are raising grandchildren affected by the opioid crisis find the resources needed to obtain financial assistance.

Heroin Epidemic Relief Organization
phone: (708) 557-8394
website: www.theherofoundation.org

Founded by Brian Kirk and John Roberts, who lost their sons to drug overdoses, this nonprofit organization aims to help families detect signs of drug abuse in their children and to help those who have lost loved ones to drug abuse cope with grief.

National Coalition Against Prescription Drug Abuse
PO Box 87
San Ramon, CA 94583
phone: (925) 480-7723
email: info@ncapda.org
website: www.ncapda.org

The National Coalition Against Prescription Drug Abuse was founded in June 2010 to help combat the opioid crisis. It partners with different institutions to find a solution and to help bring awareness to the crisis.

National Institute on Drug Abuse
Office of Science Policy and Communications
Public Information and Liaison Branch
6001 Executive Boulevard
Room 5213, MSC 9561
Bethesda, MD 20892
phone: (301) 443-1124
email: drugfacts@nida.nih.gov
website: www.drugabuse.gov

The National Institute on Drug Abuse focuses on providing clinical research on drug use to help improve the treatment of drug abuse.

Overdose Lifeline, Inc.
1100 W. 42nd Street, Suite 345
Indianapolis, IN 46208
phone: (844) 554-3354
email: contact@overdose-lifeline.org
website: www.overdose-lifeline.org

This nonprofit organization, founded in 2014, is based in Indiana and focuses on helping those addicted to drugs find the resources and assistance needed to get better. The goal of this organization is also to destigmatize the disease in order to better fight the opioid crisis.

Parents of Addicted Loved Ones (PAL)
11225 N. 28th Drive Suite B248
Phoenix, AZ 85029
phone: (480) 300-4712
email: info@palgroup.org
website: www.palgroup.org

Parents of Addicted Loved Ones (PAL) is a support group for parents who have a child suffering from substance abuse disorder. Its volunteers are comprised of parents who have the experience needed to help other parents directly affected by the drug epidemic.

Partnership for a Drug-Free New Jersey
155 Millburn Avenue
Millburn, NJ 07041
phone: (973) 467-2100
email: conover@drugfreenj.org
website: www.drugfreenj.org

Founded in 1992, this organization partners with the Governor's Council on Alcoholism and Drub Abuse and with the New Jersey Department of Human Services to provide information and resources to healthcare professionals, families, and communities to better fight drug and alcohol abuse. It also focuses on addressing the opioid crisis in New Jersey.

Partnership for Drug-Free Kids
352 Park Avenue South, 9th Floor
New York, NY 10010
phone: (212) 922-1560
website: www.drugfree.org

The Partnership for Drug-Free Kids helps parents find the resources and information they need to fight drug addiction in their households. It offers a helpline, peer support, and suggestions for treatments, among other services.

Rural Health Information Hub
School of Medicine and Health Sciences, Suite E231
1301 N. Columbia Road, Stop 9037
Grand Forks, ND 58202-9037
phone: 1 (800) 270-1898
email: info@ruralhealthinfo.org
website: www.ruralhealthinfo.org

The Rural Health Information Hub is a resource center sponsored by the Federal Office of Rural Health Policy. It is also a useful place to find information on how the opioid crisis is being addressed in rural areas.

South Central PA Opioid Awareness Coalition
phone: (717) 544-3883
email: contact@opioidaware.org
website: www.opioidaware.org

The goal of this alliance between eight counties in South Central Pennsylvania (Adams County, Cumberland County, Dauphin County, Franklin County, Fulton County, Lancaster County, Lebanon County, and York County) is to fight the rise of opioid overdoses and addiction, especially in Pennsylvania. More information is available in each respective county about local resources for drug abusers.

Substance Abuse and Mental Health Services Administration (SAMHSA)
5600 Fishers Lane
Rockville, MD 20857
phone: 1 (877) 726-4727
email: recoverymonth@samhsa.hhs.gov
website: www.samhsa.gov

This organization offers a helpline, which is available 24/7 and all year long, to help people suffering from substance abuse disorder find the help they need. It has also been at the forefront of the fight to control the opioid crisis, donating over $1 billion to the cause.

Bibliography

Books

D'Anne Burwell. *Saving Jake: When Addiction Hits Home.* Los Altos, CA: FocusUp Books, 2015.

Maureen Cavanagh. *If You Love Me: A Mother's Journey Through Her Daughter's Opioid Addiction.* New York, NY: Henry Holt and Co., 2018.

Ryan Hampton. *American Fix: Inside the Opioid Addiction Crisis—and How to End It.* New York, NY: All Points Books, 2018.

Johann Hari. *Chasing the Scream: The Opposite of Addiction is Connection.* New York, NY: Bloomsbury USA, 2015.

Anna Lembke. *Drug Dealer, MD: How Doctors Were Duped, Patients Got Hooked, and Why It's So Hard to Stop.* Baltimore, MD: Johns Hopkins University Press, 2016.

Beth Macy. *Dopesick: Dealers, doctors, and the Company That Addicted America.* New York, NY: Little, Brown and Company, 2018.

Barry Meier. *Pain Killer: An Empire of Deceit and the Origin of America's Opioid Epidemic.* New York, NY: Random House, 2018.

Sam Quinones. *Dreamland: The True Tale of America's Opiate Epidemic.* London, UK: Bloomsbury Press, 2015.

Jodee Redmond. *The Dangers of Drug Abuse.* Broomall, PA: Mason Crest, 2018.

Lloyd Sederer. *The Addiction Solution: Treating Our Dependence on Opioids and Other Drugs.* New York, NY: Scribner, 2018.

David Sheff. *Clean: Overcoming Addiction and Ending America's Greatest Tragedy.* New York, NY: Eamon Dolan/Houghton Mifflin Harcourt, 2013.

Nic Sheff. *We All Fall Down: Living with Addiction*. New York, NY: Little, Brown Books for Young Readers, 2011.

Maia Szalavitz. *Unbroken Brain: A Revolutionary New Way of Understanding Addiction*. New York, NY: St. Martin's Press, 2016.

John Temple. *American Pain: How a Young Felon and His Ring of Doctors Unleashed America's Deadliest Drug Epidemic*. New York, NY: Lyons Press, 2015.

Xina M. Uhl. *Preventing and Treating Addiction*. Broomall, PA: Mason Crest, 2017.

Periodicals and Internet Sources

Ken Alltucker, "Drug Company Raised Price of Lifesaving Opioid Overdose Antidote More Than 600 Percent," *USA Today*, November 19, 2018, https://www.usatoday.com/story/news/health/2018/11/19/kaleo-opioid-overdose-antidote-naloxone-evzio-rob-portman-medicare-medicaid/2060033002.

"America's Pill Mills: A Look into the Prescription Opioid Problem," DrugAbuse.com. October 10, 2018, https://drugabuse.com/featured/americas-pill-mills.

Marcia Angell, "Opioid Nation," *New York Review of Books*, December 6, 2018, https://www.nybooks.com/articles/2018/12/06/opioid-nation.

Kristen Bahler, "Parents are Cutting Off Their Opioid-Addicted Kids—and It's the Toughest Decision of Their Lives," *Money Magazine*, November 12. 2018, http://time.com/money/longform/parents-opioid-addiction-money-cost.

Jessica Baron, "How Technology Fails Us In the Battle Against Opioid Addiction," *Forbes*, November 6, 2018, https://www.forbes.com/sites/jessicabaron/2018/11/06/how-technology-fails-us-in-the-battle-against-opioid-addiction/#36e32f636f9b.

Lenny Bernstein, "FDA Set to Approve Potent Opioid for Market Despite Adviser's Objections," *Washington Post*, October 25, 2018, https://www. washingtonpost.com/national/health-science/fda-set-to-approve-potent-opioid-for-market-despite-advisers-objections/2018/10/25/8e3619d4-d7c2-11e8-83a2-d1c3da28d6b6_story.html?noredirect=on&utm_term=. c1220b1bd051.

Hansa D. Bhargava, "Opioid (Narcotic) Pain Medications," WebMD, September 20, 2018. Accessed September 27, 2018, https://www.webmd.com/pain-management/guide/ narcotic-pain-medications#1.

Alison Block, "A Doctor's Dilemma: Do I Prescribe Opioids?" *Washington Post*, June 10, 2016, accessed October 8, 2018, https://www.washingtonpost.com/opinions/a-doctors-dilemma-do-i-prescribe-opioids/2016/06/10/ be4bb51e-2c31-11e6-b5db-e9bc84a2c8e4_story. html?noredirect=on&utm_term=.26887a42f881.

Tao Che, "Opioids That Are Painkillers but Aren't Addictive? This Biochemist Thinks It's Possible," *CNBC*, June 22, 2018, https://www.cnbc.com/2018/06/22/ opioids-that-are-painkillers-but-arent-addictive. html?&qsearchterm=opioids.

Nick Corasaniti, "New Jersey Sues Pharmaceutical Company Amid Spiraling Opioid Crisis," *New York Times*, November 13, 2018, https://www.nytimes.com/2018/11/13/nyregion/ nj-opioid-lawsuit.html.

Kristina Davis, "Arrest Made in La Jolla Man's Fentanyl Overdose Death," *San Diego Union-Tribune*, October 10, 2018, http://www.sandiegouniontribune.com/news/courts/ sd-me-fentanyl-death-20181010-story.html.

Elana Gordon, "What's the Evidence That Supervised Drug Injection Sites Save Lives?" National Public Radio.

September 7, 2018, https://www.npr.org/sections/health-shots/2018/09/07/645609248/whats-the-evidence-that-supervised-drug-injection-sites-save-lives.

"Heroin," National Institute on Drug Abuse, June 2018, https://www.drugabuse.gov/publications/drugfacts/heroin#ref.

Josh Katz, "Drug Deaths in America Are Rising Faster Than Ever," *New York Times*, June 5, 2017, https://www.nytimes.com/interactive/2017/06/05/upshot/opioid-epidemic-drug-overdose-deaths-are-rising-faster-than-ever.html.

Steven A. King, "Opioids, Suicide, Mental Disorders, and Pain," *Psychiatric Times*, November 21, 2018, http://www.psychiatrictimes.com/psychopharmacology/opioids-suicide-mental-disorders-and-pain.

German Lopez, "Elizabeth Warren Wants Answers About Trump's 'Pathetic' Response to The Opioid Epidemic," *Vox*, July 19, 2018, https://www.vox.com/policy-and-politics/2018/7/19/17590434/elizabeth-warren-trump-opioid-epidemic.

German Lopez, "In One Year, Drug Overdoses Killed More Americans Than the Entire Vietnam War Did," *Vox*, June 8, 2017, https://www.vox.com/policy-and-politics/2017/6/6/15743986/opioid-epidemic-overdose-deaths-2016.

German Lopez, "The Opioid Epidemic, Explained," *Vox*, December 21, 2017, https://www.vox.com/science-and-health/2017/8/3/16079772/opioid-epidemic-drug-overdoses.

Pia Malbran, "What's a Pill Mill?" *CBS News*, May 31, 2007, https://www.cbsnews.com/news/whats-a-pill-mill/.

"Medications to Treat Opioid Use Disorder," National Institute on Drug Abuse, June 2018, https://www.drugabuse.gov/

publications/research-reports/medications-to-treat-opioid-addiction/overview.

Phil McCausland and Tom Winter, "China and the United States Come to Agreement at G-20 Summit Around Fentanyl," *NBC News*, December 2, 2018, https://www.nbcnews.com/news/us-news/china-united-states-come-agreement-around-fentanyl-n942766.

Chris McGreal, "The Making of an Opioid Epidemic," *Guardian*, November 8, 2018, https://www.theguardian.com/news/2018/nov/08/the-making-of-an-opioid-epidemic.

"Opioid Crisis Fast Facts," *CNN*, November 5, 2018, https://www.cnn.com/2017/09/18/health/opioid-crisis-fast-facts/index.html.

"Opioids," *Psychology Today*, February 1, 2018, https://www.psychologytoday.com/us/conditions/opioids.

David Pittman, "Facing Mounting Opioid Overdoses, Maryland Doctor Defies Federal Law," *POLITICO*, November 11, 2017, https://www.politico.com/story/2017/11/15/facing-mounting-opioid-overdoses-maryland-doctor-defies-federal-law-244948.

"President Donald J. Trump Is Taking Action on Drug Addiction and the Opioid Crisis," Whitehouse.gov, October 26. 2017, https://www.whitehouse.gov/briefings-statements/president-donald-j-trump-taking-action-drug-addiction-opioid-crisis.

Sara Randazzo, "Opioid Industry Fights Efforts to Make It Pay for Crisis," *Wall Street Journal*, November 19, 2018, https://www.wsj.com/articles/opioid-industry-takes-new-york-to-court-over-new-levy-1542623400.

Krista Rossi, "Facing Regional, Financial and Access Hurdles in Opioid Addiction," *MD Magazine*, October 27, 2018, https://www.mdmag.com/medical-news/facing-regional-financial-access-hurdles-opioid-addiction.

Terry Spencer, "Florida Sues CVS, Walgreens Over Opioid Sales," *Boston Globe,* November 18, 2018, https://www.bostonglobe.com/business/2018/11/17/florida-sues-cvs-walgreens-over-opioid-sales/6bL8FXyi7bZPVC24QYlviP/story.html.

Yvette C. Terrie, "An Overview of Opioids," *Pharmacy Times*, June 13, 2011, https://www.pharmacytimes.com/publications/issue/2011/june2011/an-overview-of-opioids.

Index